The Ultimate Austrian Cookbook

111 Dishes From Austria To Cook Right Now

Slavka Bodic

Imprint: Independently published

Please sign up for free Balkan and Mediterranean recipes:
www.balkanfood.org

Introduction

Austrian cuisine is known for its hearty dishes and sweet pastries. Some of its signature dishes include Wiener Schnitzel (breaded and fried veal), Kaiserschmarrn (a fluffy caramelized pancake), and Tafelspitz (boiled beef with horseradish sauce). Additionally, the country is famous for its pastries and desserts, such as Apfelstrudel (apple strudel) and Sachertorte (a rich chocolate cake). The use of high-quality ingredients and traditional cooking methods also add to the appeal of Austrian cuisine.

The Ultimate Austrian Cookbook will introduce to Austrian cuisine and its culinary culture in a way that you may have never learn before. It brings you a variety of Austrian recipes in one place. The cookbook is perfect for all those who are always keen to cook healthy food and want to try new and unique flavors. With the help of this Austrian cuisine cookbook, you can create a complete Austrian menu at home, you can try all the special Austrian recipes on your special occasions and celebrations. In this cookbook, you'll find popular Austrian meals and the ones that you might not have heard of. From nourishing cevapi for breakfast to all of the warming meat stews and soups, the Austrian desserts, drinks, the entrees, and healthy Austrian salads, etc., you can find them all. And all these recipes are created in such a simple way that those who aren't even familiar with the Austrian culture, food, and language can still try and cook them at home without facing much difficulty.

Austrian culinary culture and cuisine are indeed full of wonders. There's a great use of meat, veggies like okra and eggplants, etc., and other spices. And, if you want to add all those nutria-dense ingredients to your routine diet, then give this book a thorough read, and you'll find all your answers right away.

What you can find in this cookbook:

- ➤ Facts about Austria and Austrian Cuisine
- ➤ Austrian Breakfast Recipes
- ➤ The Snacks, Sides, or Appetizers
- ➤ Soups and Salads
- ➤ Main Dishes and Entrees
- ➤ Austrian Desserts and Drinks

Let's try all these Austrian Recipes and recreate a complete menu to celebrate the amazing Austrian flavors and aromas!

TABLE OF CONTENTS

Why Austrian Cuisine?

Austrian cuisine has its roots in the Habsburg Empire, which ruled over a large part of Europe for several centuries. The cuisine was influenced by the cuisine of neighboring countries, such as Germany, Hungary, Italy, and the Czech Republic, as well as by the traditional cuisine of the country's rural population. The empire's multicultural makeup also led to the integration of various regional and ethnic cuisines, resulting in a diverse and rich culinary tradition. In addition, Austria's historical position as a crossroads of trade and travel further contributed to the development of its cuisine. Austrian cuisine is also known for its pastries and sweets, such as Sachertorte (a rich chocolate cake) and Linzer Torte (a jam-filled pastry with a lattice crust). Some of the other famous Austrian dishes include:

Wiener Schnitzel

Wiener Schnitzel is a traditional Austrian dish made from thin slices of veal that are breaded and fried until crispy. The veal is pounded thin, then coated in flour, beaten eggs, and breadcrumbs before being fried in oil or butter. The dish is served with a simple lemon wedge and is often accompanied by potatoes or a salad. Wiener Schnitzel is considered to be Austria's national dish and is popular throughout the country and beyond. The dish is so closely associated with Austria that the term "Wiener" in "Wiener Schnitzel" is protected by EU law and can only be used to describe dishes made from veal. Similar dishes made with pork or chicken are known as "Schnitzel" but not "Wiener Schnitzel."

Tafelspitz

Tafelspitz is a traditional Austrian dish made from boiled beef, usually from the top round, served with a sauce made from the cooking liquid, fresh horseradish, and sometimes apples. It is a popular dish in Austria and is often served as a Sunday meal with boiled potatoes and a side of creamed spinach. The dish is named after the "Tafel", meaning "table" in German, and "Spitz," meaning "point" in reference to the cut of beef used. The cooking process and tenderness of the meat result in a flavorful and juicy dish that is highly regarded in Austrian cuisine.

Kaiserschmarrn

Kaiserschmarrn is a traditional Austrian dish made from shredded pancakes that are caramelized in sugar and served with a fruit compote, such as plum, apple or raspberry. The pancakes are made from a light batter of eggs, sugar, flour, and milk, which are then fried and torn into pieces. The sugar caramelizes in the pan and creates a sweet and crunchy crust on the pieces of pancake. Kaiserschmarrn is often served as a dessert and is a staple in Austrian cuisine, especially in the Alpine regions. The dish is said to have been a favorite of the Austro-Hungarian Emperor Franz Joseph I, and is named after him as "Kaiserschmarrn."

Austria

The country is surrounded by the beautiful Alpine mountain range, which provides a picturesque backdrop to the picturesque cities, towns, and villages of Austria. The capital of Austria is Vienna, which is also its largest city. Vienna is known for its grand architecture, sophisticated culture, and rich musical heritage. The city was once the center of the Habsburg Empire and played a major role in the history of Europe. Today, Vienna is home to numerous museums, galleries, and cultural institutions, as well as some of the world's most famous concert halls and opera houses.

Austria has a rich cultural heritage, reflected in its architecture, art, music, and cuisine. The country is known for its beautiful Baroque palaces, Gothic cathedrals, and Renaissance castles, which are a testament to its rich history. Austrian cuisine is hearty and flavorful, often featuring dishes made with meat and potatoes, as well as famous pastries and sweets such as Sachertorte and Apfelstrudel.

Austria is known for its stunning natural landscapes, which include rolling hills, snow-capped mountains, crystal-clear lakes, and pristine forests. The country is located in the heart of Europe and is surrounded by the majestic Alpine mountain range, which provides a picturesque backdrop to the picturesque cities, towns, and villages of Austria.

One of the most famous natural landmarks in Austria is the Grossglockner, which is the highest mountain in the country and a popular destination for hikers and mountaineers. The country is also home to numerous other peaks, including the Hohe Tauern, the Karwendel, and the Rieserferner, which offer breathtaking views of the surrounding landscapes.

In addition to its mountain landscapes, Austria is also known for its scenic lakes and rivers. The country is home to numerous pristine lakes, such as Lake Constance, Lake Geneva, and Lake Mondsee, which are popular for swimming, boating, and fishing. The country's many rivers, including the Danube, Inn, and Mur, also provide opportunities for rafting, kayaking, and canoeing.

Austria's forests and parks are another highlight of its natural landscape. The country is home to numerous forests and parks, including the Vienna Woods, the Neusiedler See-Seewinkel National Park, and the High Tauern National Park, which offer a range of recreational activities, including hiking, cycling, and wildlife watching. Austria is also known for its thriving winter sports industry, with ski resorts located throughout the country, especially in the Alps. The country has hosted numerous winter Olympic Games, and many of the world's top skiers and snowboarders come to Austria to train and compete.

Breakfast

Viennese Apfelstrudel

Preparation time: 10 minutes

Cook time: 45 minutes

Nutrition facts (per serving): 387 Cal (20g fat, 7g protein, 4g fiber)

Viennese Apfelstrudel is a traditional Austrian dessert made of a thin, flaky pastry dough filled with cooked and spiced apples. The dough is stretched out by hand into a thin sheet, then the apples are placed on top and the whole thing is rolled up into a spiral shape.

Ingredients (8 Servings)

Dough

3 cups all-purpose flour

¼ cup warm water

1 egg

¼ cup butter, melted

¼ cup sour cream

Filling

2 lbs. Granny Smith apples (about 6-7 apples)

½ cup granulated sugar

1 teaspoon cinnamon

¼ cup raisins (optional)

¼ cup breadcrumbs

¼ cup butter, melted

Preparation

To make the prepared dough, combine the flour, warm water, egg, melted butter, and sour cream in a suitable-sized mixing bowl. Knead this dough until a smooth and elastic dough forms. Cover the prepared dough with a kitchen towel and let it rest for at least 30 minutes. To make the filling, peel and core the apples, then slice them thinly. In a suitable-sized mixing bowl, combine the apples, sugar, cinnamon, raisins (if using), breadcrumbs, and melted butter. Mix well. Roll out the prepared dough on a floured surface into a large rectangle, about ⅛ inch thick. Spread the apple filling over the prepared dough, leaving about 2 inches of empty space at the edges. Roll up the prepared dough tightly, starting from the long side, to form a large strudel. Pinch the edges to seal. Place the prepared strudel on a baking sheet and brush it with melted butter. Bake in a preheated oven at 350 degrees F for about 45 minutes, or until golden brown and crispy. Slice and serve after cooling.

Tiroler Omelette

Preparation time: 10 minutes
Cook time: 6 minutes
Nutrition facts (per serving): 218 Cal (10g fat, 22g protein, 5g fiber)

Tiroler Omelette, also known as "Kaiserschmarrn," is a traditional dish from the Tyrol region in Austria. Here's a sweet and fluffy omelette that's typically served with a fruit compote or a warm caramel sauce.

Ingredients (4 Servings)

4 eggs
¼ cup granulated sugar
¼ cup flour
¼ cup milk
1 teaspoon vanilla extract
¼ teaspoon salt
2 tablespoons butter
Powdered sugar, for dusting

Preparation

In a suitable-sized mixing bowl, whisk together the eggs, sugar, flour, milk, vanilla extract, and salt. Heat a suitable skillet over medium heat and add the butter. Pour the egg mixture into the skillet and cook, stirring occasionally, until the omelette is set and golden brown. Once the omelette is cooked, tear it into large chunks with a fork or a pair of tongs. Cook the omelette chunks for an additional 2-3 minutes, or until crispy and golden brown. Serve the Tiroler Omelette warm, dusted with powdered sugar and with a fruit compote or caramel sauce.

Apfelradln

Preparation time: 10 minutes
Cook time: 40 minutes
Nutrition facts (per serving): 274 Cal (11g fat, 7g protein, 6g fiber)

Also known as "Apfelradel" or "Apfelrolle," is a traditional dish from Austria that's made with apples wrapped in a pastry dough. The apples are typically peeled, cored and sliced before being wrapped in the prepared dough and then fried or baked.

Ingredients (4-6 Servings)
4-6 apples, peeled, cored and sliced
½ cup granulated sugar
1 teaspoon cinnamon
¼ cup raisins (optional)
¼ cup breadcrumbs
¼ cup butter, melted
1 sheet of puff pastry or strudel dough
Powdered sugar, for dusting

Preparation
At 350 degrees F, preheat your oven. In a suitable-sized mixing bowl, combine the apples, sugar, cinnamon, raisins (if using), breadcrumbs, and melted butter. Mix well. Roll out the puff pastry or strudel dough on a floured surface into a large rectangle, about ⅛ inch thick. Place the apple mixture on one half of the prepared dough, leaving about 2 inches of empty space at the edges. Fold the other half of the prepared dough

over the apples and press the edges together to seal. Place the Apfelradln on a baking sheet and brush it with melted butter. Bake in the preheated oven for about 30-40 minutes, or until golden brown and crispy. Remove this dish from the oven and let it cool before dusting with powdered sugar and slicing.

Austrian Crepes (Palatschinken)

Preparation time: 10 minutes
Cook time: 10 minutes
Nutrition facts (per serving): 287 Cal (8g fat, 4g protein, 2.4g fiber)

Palatschinken is a traditional Austrian dish similar to crepes, typically filled with fruit, jam, or Nutella.

Ingredients (6 Servings)
1 cup of flour
2 large eggs
1 cup of milk
2 tablespoons of sugar
Pinch of salt
2 tablespoons of melted butter
Butter or oil, for frying

Preparation
In a suitable-sized mixing bowl, whisk together the flour, eggs, milk, sugar, salt, and melted butter until smooth. Heat a small amount of butter or oil in a non-stick pan over medium heat. Add a small amount of batter into the pan and swirl to coat the bottom evenly. Cook until the top of the Palatschinke is set and the bottom is lightly browned, about 2-3 minutes. Flip this crepe and continue cooking the other side until lightly browned, another minute or two. Repeat with the remaining

batter, adding more butter or oil as needed. Serve the Palatschinken warm, filled with your choice of fruit, jam, or Nutella. Enjoy!

Tiroler Gröstl

Preparation time: 10 minutes
Cook time: 10 minutes
Nutrition facts (per serving): 322 Cal (10g fat, 20g protein, 1.4g fiber)

Tiroler Gröstl is a traditional dish from the Tyrol region in Austria. It's a hearty dish made from pan-fried potatoes, bacon and onions, and typically served with a fried or poached egg on top.

Ingredients (2 Servings)
1 lb. potatoes, peeled and diced
1 onion, finely chopped
4 slices of bacon, diced
¼ cup butter
Black pepper and salt, to taste
4 eggs (optional)

Preparation
In a suitable pot, boil the potatoes until they are tender. Drain and set aside. In a suitable skillet, melt the butter over medium heat. Add the diced bacon and onions and cook until the bacon is crispy and the onions are translucent. Add the cooked potatoes to the skillet and stir to combine. Season with black pepper and salt. Cook the potato mixture for an additional 2-3 minutes, or until the potatoes are crispy and golden brown. If desired, fry or poach the eggs and place one on top of each serving of Tiroler Gröstl. Serve the Tiroler Gröstl hot as a main dish.

Weisses Rössl

Preparation time: 10 minutes
Cook time: 9 minutes
Nutrition facts (per serving): 301 Cal (9g fat, 21g protein, 1.2g fiber)

Weißes Rössl is a traditional dish from Austria and Germany, it's made by sautéing veal or pork cutlets with a white wine and cream sauce. It is mostly served with a side of spaetzle or rosti and a green salad.

Ingredients (4 Servings)

4 veal or pork cutlets
Black pepper and salt, to taste
¼ cup flour
2 tablespoons butter
½ cup white wine
½ cup heavy cream
1 tablespoon chopped parsley, optional

Preparation

Season the cutlets with black pepper and salt and coat in flour. In a suitable skillet, melt the butter over medium-high heat. Add the cutlets to the skillet and cook for 2-3 minutes on each side, or until golden brown. Remove the prepared cutlets from the skillet and set aside. Add the white wine to the skillet and bring to a simmer, scraping the bottom of the pan to release any browned bits. Stir in the heavy cream and bring the prepared mixture to a simmer. Return the cutlets to the skillet and spoon the sauce over them. Continue cooking for an additional 2-3 minutes, or until the sauce has thickened and the cutlets are cooked through. Sprinkle with chopped parsley, if desired. Serve the Weißes Rössl with spaetzle or rosti and a green salad.

Kaiserschmarrn

Preparation time: 10 minutes
Cook time: 6 minutes
Nutrition facts (per serving): 249 Cal (8g fat, 9g protein, 4g fiber)

Kaiserschmarrn is a traditional and popular dish from Austria; here's a type of pancakes made from shredded pancakes and served with a sweet fruit compote or caramelized fruit.

Ingredients (4 Servings)
4 eggs, separated
½ cup all-purpose flour
½ cup milk
2 tablespoons sugar
¼ teaspoon salt
2 tablespoons butter
Powdered sugar, for dusting
Fruit compote or caramelized fruit, to serve

Preparation
In a suitable-sized mixing bowl, whisk together the egg yolks, flour, milk, sugar, and salt until smooth. In another suitable bowl, beat the egg whites until stiff peaks form. Add the egg whites into the prepared batter until just combined. In a suitable skillet, melt the butter over medium-high heat. Add the flour batter into the skillet and cook for 2-3 minutes until the bottom is golden. Use forks to shred the half-cooked pancake into bite-sized pieces. Continue cooking the shredded pancake for an

additional 2-3 minutes, or until golden brown and crispy on all sides. Sprinkle powdered sugar over the top and serve with fruit compote or caramelized fruit.

Austrian Egg Spätzle

Preparation time: 10 minutes
Cook time: 10 minutes
Nutrition facts (per serving): 217 Cal (3g fat, 10g protein, 2g fiber)

Spätzle is a traditional egg noodle dish from Austria and Germany. It's made by mixing eggs, flour and water to create a dough which is then extruded or scraped into boiling water. It's mostly served as a side dish with meat dishes.

Ingredients (4 Servings)

2 cups all-purpose flour

½ teaspoon salt

4 eggs

½ cup water

2 tablespoons butter (optional)

Chopped parsley (optional)

Preparation

In a suitable-sized mixing bowl, combine the flour and salt. In another bowl, whisk together the eggs and water. Gradually add the egg mixture to the flour mixture, stirring until a smooth and elastic dough forms. Allow the prepared dough to rest for at least 30 minutes. Bring a suitable pot of salted water to a boil. Using a spätzle press, potato ricer or a colander with large holes, press or scrape the prepared dough into the boiling water. Cook the spätzle for 2-3 minutes, or until they float to the surface. Use a slotted spoon to remove the spätzle from the water and drain them well.

Optional

In a suitable skillet, melt the butter over medium heat. Add the cooked spätzle and toss to coat them in the butter. Serve the Spätzle hot, garnished with chopped parsley if desired.

Quark Käse

Preparation time: 10 minutes
Nutrition facts (per serving): 238 Cal (23g fat, 7g protein, 3g fiber)

Quark is a type of fresh cheese that is popular in German and Austrian cuisine. It's made by curdling milk with rennet or a souring agent. It has a nice smooth texture and a mild, slightly tangy flavor.

Ingredients (6 Servings)
1 gallon whole milk
¼ cup buttermilk
Salt, to taste

Preparation
In a suitable pot, heat the milk over medium heat until it reaches a temperature of around 86-90°F (30-32°C). Remove this milk pot from heat and stir in the buttermilk. Cover the pot and let it sit at room temperature for 12-24 hours, or until the milk has thickened and curdled. Line any suitable colander with a cheesecloth and place it over a suitable-sized bowl. Pour the curdled milk into the colander to strain the liquid whey. Bring all the edges of the cheesecloth together and tie them together to form a bundle. Hang the bundle from a wooden spoon or a metal hook set over a bowl to continue draining for several hours or overnight. Once the cheese is drained to your desired consistency, unwrap the cheese and transfer it to a container. Add salt to taste and stir it in. Cover the container and refrigerate the quark for at least 24 hours before serving, it will keep for up to a week in the refrigerator.

Buchteln Mit Vanillesauce

Preparation time: 10 minutes
Cook time: 35 minutes
Nutrition facts (per serving): 352 Cal (22g fat, 8g protein, 2g fiber)

Buchteln are a type of sweet yeast dumplings that are popular in many Central European countries, including Austria. They're often filled with jam or poppy seeds, and served with a vanilla sauce.

Ingredients (6 Servings)
Dough
1 cup milk
2 ¼ teaspoon active dry yeast
¼ cup sugar
¼ cup butter, melted
1 egg
3 cups all-purpose flour
¼ teaspoon salt

Filling
½ cup jam or poppy seed filling

Vanilla Sauce
1 cup milk
½ cup heavy cream
½ cup sugar
1 vanilla bean, split and scraped
2 egg yolks
1 tablespoon cornstarch

Preparation

In a suitable saucepan, heat the milk until lukewarm. Remove from heat and stir in the yeast and 1 tablespoon of sugar. Let the prepared mixture sit for about 10 minutes, or until it becomes frothy. In a suitable-sized mixing bowl, combine the flour, remaining sugar, and salt. Add the yeast mixture, melted butter, and egg to the flour mixture and stir until a smooth dough forms. Knead the prepared dough for about 5-7 minutes, or until it becomes smooth and elastic. Place the prepared dough in a greased bowl and cover it with a clean kitchen towel. Leave it to rise in a warm place for about 1 hour, or until it doubles in size. At 350 degrees F, preheat your oven. Roll out the prepared dough on a floured surface to about ¼ inch thickness. Spread the filling over the prepared dough, leaving a small border around the edges. Roll up the prepared dough and cut it into slices about 1 inch thick. Spread the slices in a greased baking dish and let them rise for another 20-30 minutes. Bake the buchteln for about 20-25 minutes, or until they're golden brown.

Vanilla Sauce

In a suitable saucepan over medium heat, combine the milk, cream, sugar, and vanilla bean. Bring the prepared mixture to a simmer. In a suitable-sized bowl, whisk together the egg yolks and cornstarch. Slowly pour the prepared egg mixture into the saucepan, whisking constantly to prevent curdling. Continue to cook the prepared mixture over medium heat, stirring constantly, until it thickens. Remove from heat and strain the sauce through a fine-mesh sieve. Let it cool before serving it with the Buchteln.

Austrian Scrambled Eggs

Preparation time: 10 minutes
Cook time: 10 minutes
Nutrition facts (per serving): 216 Cal (20g fat, 20g protein, 3g fiber)

Austrian Scrambled Eggs, also known as "Rührei," is a traditional and simple dish that's typically served as a breakfast or brunch option.

Ingredients (2 Servings)
4 eggs
2 tablespoons butter
Diced ham, to taste
Herbs or cheese, to taste
Black pepper and salt, to taste

Preparation
Add eggs to a suitable bowl and beat them with a fork or whisk until the yolks and whites are fully combined. Season the eggs with black pepper and salt. In a suitable pan over medium heat, melt the butter. Once the butter is hot, pour in the eggs and stir them constantly with a rubber spatula. As the eggs start to cook, you can add diced ham, herbs, or cheese if desired. Keep stirring until the eggs are fully cooked and reach your desired consistency. Serve the scrambled eggs immediately with bread or with a side of sautéed vegetables.

Austrian Hash

Preparation time: 10 minutes
Cook time: 6 minutes
Nutrition facts (per serving): 299 Cal (20g fat, 8g protein, 2.4g fiber)

"Kartoffelrosti" or Austrian hash is a traditional dish that's made from grated potatoes and is typically served as a side dish or breakfast dish.

Ingredients (4 Servings)

3-4 large potatoes, peeled and grated
1 small onion, grated
1 egg
¼ cup flour
Vegetable oil, for frying
Black pepper and salt, to taste

Preparation

In a suitable-sized bowl, combine the grated potatoes, grated onion, egg, flour, black pepper and salt. Mix well. Heat a suitable skillet over medium heat and add enough vegetable oil to cover the bottom of the pan. Form the potato mixture into small patties, about ½ inch thick. Carefully place the patties into the hot oil and fry for about 2-3 minutes per side, or until golden brown and crispy. Drain the hash on paper towels to remove excess oil. Serve the Kartoffelrosti immediately with a side of sour cream or apple sauce or a fried egg or with a slice of bacon.

Sweet Austrian Yeast Buns Filled with a Chocolate Egg

Preparation time: 10 minutes
Cook time: 20 minutes
Nutrition facts (per serving): 318 Cal (16g fat, 7g protein, 1.8g fiber)

The sweet Austrian yeast buns filled with chocolate egg you are referring to are called "Easter Buns" or "Osterpinzen," which is a traditional Easter sweet bread from Austria.

Ingredients (4 Servings)

1 cup milk

2 tablespoons sugar

2 ¼ teaspoon active dry yeast

3 ½ cups all-purpose flour

1 teaspoon salt

2 eggs

¼ cup butter, at room temperature

Chocolate Easter eggs

1 egg yolk, beaten

Powdered sugar for dusting

Preparation

In a saucepan, heat the milk until warm. Remove from heat and stir in sugar and yeast. Let sit for about 10 minutes, or until the prepared mixture becomes frothy. In a suitable-sized bowl, combine the flour and salt. In another rightly-sized bowl, beat the eggs and then add to the flour mixture along with the yeast mixture and butter. Mix until a dough forms. Knead the prepared dough on a floured surface for about 8-10 minutes, or until it becomes smooth and elastic. Place the prepared dough in a greased bowl, cover with plastic wrap, and let it rise in a warm place for about 1 hour, or until doubled in size. At 350 degrees F, preheat your oven. Roll out the prepared dough to about ¼ inch thickness. Cut the prepared dough into circles using a round cutter or a glass. Place a chocolate Easter egg in the center of each circle, then pull the edges of the prepared dough up around the chocolate to form a bun. Place the prepared buns on a baking sheet lined with parchment paper. Brush the top of the buns with the beaten egg yolk. Bake the buns for about 15-20 minutes, or until golden brown. Let the buns cool for a few minutes, then dust with powdered sugar before serving.

Snacks and Appetizers

Austrian Lobster Cocktail

Preparation time: 10 minutes
Nutrition facts (per serving): 264 Cal (19g fat, 12g protein, 5g fiber)

An Austrian Lobster Cocktail, also known as "Langustencocktail," is a traditional dish that's made from lobster meat and served as an appetizer or a main dish.

Ingredients (2 Servings)

1 lb. cooked lobster meat
¼ cup mayonnaise
1 tablespoon ketchup
1 tablespoon lemon juice
1 tablespoon chopped fresh dill
Black pepper, to taste
Salt, to taste
Lettuce leaves, to taste
Lemon wedges, to taste

Preparation

Cut the cooked lobster meat into small bite-sized pieces. In a suitable-sized bowl, mix together the mayonnaise, ketchup, lemon juice, chopped dill, black pepper and salt. Add the lobster meat to the bowl and toss to coat with the sauce. Line a serving dish with lettuce leaves. Spoon the lobster mixture onto the lettuce leaves. Garnish with lemon wedges. Serve chilled.

Liptauer

Preparation time: 10 minutes
Nutrition facts (per serving): 188 Cal (22g fat, 11g protein, 2.4g fiber)

Liptauer is a traditional Austrian cheese spread made from a combination of sheep's milk cheese, sour cream, and various spices and herbs. It's typically served as a spread on bread or crackers, and is a popular appetizer or snack.

Ingredients (2 Servings)

8 oz sheep's milk cheese (quark or cottage cheese can be substituted)
½ cup sour cream
2 tablespoons unsalted butter, at room temperature
1 tablespoon diced onion
1 tablespoon diced pickled gherkin
1 tablespoon diced paprika pepper
2 teaspoon caraway seeds
1 teaspoon Dijon mustard
Black pepper, to taste
Salt, to taste

Preparation

In a suitable-sized mixing bowl, combine the sheep's milk cheese, sour cream, butter, onion, pickled gherkin, paprika pepper, caraway seeds, mustard, salt, and pepper. Mix well until smooth and well combined. Taste and adjust seasoning if necessary. Cover this bowl and refrigerate it for at least 30 minutes to allow the flavors to develop. Serve chilled on bread or crackers as an appetizer.

Brettljause

Preparation time: 10 minutes
Nutrition facts (per serving): 349 Cal (25g fat, 29g protein, 1.1g fiber)

Brettljause is a traditional Austrian platter of cured meats, cheese, and other snacks, usually served as an appetizer or light meal. It's a popular dish in Austria, and you can find it in most of the traditional restaurants or inns.

Ingredients (2 Servings)

¼ lb. assorted cured meats (such as ham, bacon, salami, and sausage)
¼ lb. assorted cheeses (such as Emmentaler, Gouda, and smoked cheese)
½ cup bread or crackers
½ cup pickles or pickled vegetables
¼ cup mustard or other dips
2 tablespoons fresh herbs (such as parsley or chives)

Preparation

Arrange the cured meats, cheeses, bread or crackers, pickles or pickled vegetables, and herbs on a large platter. Serve the platter with mustard or other dips on the side. You can also add some fruits and nuts to your platter.

Waldviertler Mohnzelten

Preparation time: 10 minutes
Cook time: 30 minutes
Nutrition facts (per serving): 351 Cal (7g fat, 7g protein, 1.3g fiber)

Waldviertler Mohnzelten is a traditional Austrian pastry made from a sweet dough filled with a poppy seed filling. It is a popular pastry in the Waldviertel region of Austria and is typically served as a dessert or a snack.

Ingredients (6 Servings)
Dough
1 lb. flour

10 oz. sugar

10 oz. butter

1 egg

¼ cup milk

1 teaspoon baking powder

Poppy Seed Filling
1 lb. poppy seeds

10 oz. sugar

10 oz. milk

2 eggs

1 tablespoon vanilla extract

Powdered sugar, for dusting

Preparation

To make the prepared dough, combine the flour, sugar, butter, egg, milk and baking powder in a suitable-sized mixing bowl. Knead the prepared dough until it becomes smooth and elastic. Cover the prepared dough and let it rest in the refrigerator for at least 30 minutes. To make the filling, grind the poppy seeds in a food processor or a spice grinder. In a medium saucepan, combine the ground poppy seeds, sugar, milk, eggs, and vanilla extract. Cook this mixture over medium heat, stirring constantly, until the prepared mixture thickens. Remove from heat and let it cool. At 350 degrees F, preheat your oven. Roll out the prepared dough on a floured surface to about 3mm thickness. Spread the poppy seed filling evenly over the prepared dough, leaving a 1 inch border around the edges. Roll up the prepared dough tightly, starting from the long side. Cut the roll into slices about 2-3 cm thick. Place the slices on a baking sheet lined with parchment paper. Bake for 25-30 minutes, or until golden brown. Remove from oven and let cool. Dust with powdered sugar before serving.

Belegte Brote

Preparation time: 10 minutes
Nutrition facts (per serving): 322 Cal (12g fat, 11g protein, 4g fiber)

Belegte Brote is a German dish that translates to "filled sandwiches." Here's a type of sandwich made by spreading a variety of toppings, such as cheese, meat, vegetables, or condiments, on slices of bread. Belegte Brote is a popular lunch or snack food in Germany, and can be found in many cafes, bakeries, and snack bars.

Ingredients (4 Servings)

4 slices of bread (e.g. sourdough, rye)
Mayonnaise, to taste
Dijon mustard, to taste
4 thin slices of cooked ham
4 thin slices of cheese (e.g. Emmental, Gouda)
4-8 slices of tomato
4-8 leaves of lettuce
Salt, to taste
Black pepper, to taste

Preparation

Toast the slices of bread. Spread a thin layer of mayonnaise on each slice of bread. Spread a thin layer of Dijon mustard on top of the mayonnaise. Place a slice of ham on each slice of bread. Add a slice of cheese over the ham. Place the slices of tomato and lettuce on top of the cheese. Season them well with black pepper and salt to taste. Serve open-faced and enjoy!

Austrian Apricot Dumplings

Preparation time: 10 minutes

Cook time: 15 minutes

Nutrition facts (per serving): 192 Cal (1g fat, 5g protein, 4g fiber)

Apricot dumplings, or Marillenknödel in German, are a traditional Austrian dish made with a dumpling dough filled with apricot jam, and usually served with a butter, breadcrumbs, and sugar topping.

Ingredients (6 Servings)

Dough

10 oz. flour

1 egg

¼ cup milk

1 teaspoon salt

Filling

12 apricot halves in syrup

1 tablespoon breadcrumbs

Topping

2 tablespoons butter

2 tablespoons breadcrumbs

2 tablespoons sugar

Water, for boiling

Preparation

To make the prepared dough, mix together the flour, egg, milk, and salt in a suitable-sized mixing bowl until a smooth dough forms. Knead the prepared dough on a floured surface for a few minutes. Cover the prepared dough and let it rest for at least 30 minutes. To make the filling, drain the apricot halves and remove the pits. Mix the apricot halves with 1 tablespoon of breadcrumbs. Roll out the prepared dough on a floured surface to about ⅛ inch (3 mm) thickness. Cut the prepared dough into circles about 3 inch in diameter. Place an apricot half in the center of each dough circle. Pinch the edges of the prepared dough together to seal the apricot inside. Bring a suitable pot of water to a boil. Gently drop the dumplings into the boiling water and cook for about 10-15 minutes. To make the topping, melt the butter in a suitable pan over medium heat. Add the breadcrumbs and sugar and stir until the prepared mixture is golden brown. Remove the dumplings from the water and let them drain. Roll the dumplings in the topping mixture. Serve the dumplings warm with a sprinkle of powdered sugar.

Stuffed Vienna Bread

Preparation time: 10 minutes
Cook time: 35 minutes
Nutrition facts (per serving): 278 Cal (4g fat, 10g protein, 3g fiber)

Stuffed Vienna Bread, or "Füllungsbrötchen" in German, is a traditional Austrian dish that's typically filled with different types of meats, cheeses, and vegetables.

Ingredients (6 Servings)

1 Vienna bread loaf
4-5 slices of cooked ham
4-5 slices of cooked bacon
4-5 slices of cooked salami
4-5 slices of cooked turkey
4-5 slices of gouda cheese
4-5 slices of cheddar cheese
1 small onion, finely chopped
1 small red bell pepper, finely chopped
2 cloves of garlic, minced
2 tablespoons butter
Black pepper and salt, to taste

Preparation

At 350 degrees F, preheat your oven. Cut the Vienna bread loaf lengthwise, but not all the way through, leaving the bottom intact. In a suitable pan, melt the butter and sauté the onion, red bell pepper, and garlic until they are soft. Season the vegetables with black pepper and salt. Stuff the Vienna bread with the cooked meat, cheese, and sautéed vegetables. Wrap the Vienna bread with aluminum foil and bake it in the oven for about 20-25 minutes. Uncover the dish and bake for an additional 10 minutes, or until the cheese is melted and the bread is golden brown. Slice the Vienna bread and serve it warm.

Wiener Schnitzel

Preparation time: 10 minutes
Cook time: 6 minutes
Nutrition facts (per serving): 362 Cal (2g fat, 6g protein, 1.2g fiber)

Here's a traditional Austrian dish that consists of a thin, breaded and pan-fried veal cutlet.

Ingredients (4 Servings)
4 veal cutlets, pounded thin
1 cup all-purpose flour
2 eggs, beaten
1 cup breadcrumbs
Black pepper, to taste
Salt, to taste
½ cup vegetable oil
Lemon wedges, for serving

Preparation
Season the veal cutlets with black pepper and salt. Add all-purpose flour, eggs, and breadcrumbs in three separate shallow dishes. Dredge the veal cutlets in the flour, shaking off any excess. Dip them in the beaten eggs, then coat them in the breadcrumbs, pressing the breadcrumbs onto the cutlets. Heat the oil in a suitable skillet over medium-high heat. Add the cutlets to the skillet and cook them for 2-3 minutes per side, or until they are golden brown and cooked through. Remove the cutlets from the skillet and place them on a paper towel-lined plate to drain any excess oil. Serve the Wiener Schnitzel with lemon wedges and a side of your choice, such as potato salad or roasted potatoes.

Lebkuchen Biscuits

Preparation time: 10 minutes
Cook time: 15 minutes
Nutrition facts (per serving): 243 Cal (10g fat, 4g protein, 2.4g fiber)

Lebkuchen Biscuits, also known as "Lebkuchen" in German, are a traditional German and Austrian Christmas treat. They're similar to gingerbread and often shaped into a heart shape.

Ingredients (6 Servings)
10 ½ oz. honey
3 ½ oz. brown sugar
3 ½ oz. butter
1 egg
1 lb. all-purpose flour
1 teaspoon ground cinnamon
1 teaspoon ground ginger
1 teaspoon ground nutmeg
1 teaspoon ground cloves
2 teaspoon baking powder
1 teaspoon baking soda
2 teaspoon vanilla extract
1 teaspoon grated lemon zest
Icing sugar, for dusting

Preparation

At 350 degrees F, preheat your oven. In a saucepan, combine the honey, brown sugar and butter over low heat. Cook until the sugar has dissolved and the prepared mixture is smooth. Remove this pan from heat and let it cool for a few minutes. In a suitable-sized mixing bowl, whisk together the flour, cinnamon, ginger, nutmeg, cloves, baking powder, and baking soda. Once the honey mixture has cooled slightly, add the egg, vanilla extract, and grated lemon zest. Whisk together. Gradually add the dry ingredients to the wet mixture and stir until a dough forms. Roll out the prepared dough on a floured surface to about ⅕ inch thickness. Cut out the prepared dough into desired shapes, such as hearts. Place the Lebkuchen biscuits on a baking sheet lined with parchment paper. Bake the biscuits for 12-15 minutes or until golden brown. Remove the biscuits from the oven and let them cool on a wire rack. Once cooled, dust them with icing sugar.

Spargel

Preparation time: 10 minutes
Cook time: 10 minutes
Nutrition facts (per serving): 356 Cal (13g fat, 4g protein, 7g fiber)

Spargel is a German word that refers to white asparagus, a variety of asparagus that's grown underground and is prized for its delicate flavor and tender texture. In German cuisine, Spargel is often enjoyed during the spring months and is considered a delicacy. It's typically cooked by boiling or steaming and is often served with melted butter, hollandaise sauce, or other sauces.

Ingredients (4 Servings)
2 lbs. of fresh white asparagus
Salt, to taste
2 tablespoons of butter
1 lemon, juiced
Black pepper, to taste
2 tablespoons of chopped fresh parsley, optional

Preparation
Rinse the asparagus and snap off the tough ends. Fill a suitable saucepan with about 2 inches of water and cook to a boil. Add salt to taste. Add the snapped asparagus to the boiling water and cook for 3-5 minutes, or until tender but still crisp. Drain the asparagus and transfer to a serving dish. Add the butter to the saucepan and heat until melted. Pour the melted butter over the asparagus and sprinkle with lemon juice. Season

them well with salt and black pepper to taste. Garnish with chopped fresh parsley, if desired. Serve hot and enjoy!

Linzer Tarts

Preparation time: 10 minutes
Cook time: 25 minutes
Nutrition facts (per serving): 278 Cal (22g fat, 5g protein, 4g fiber)

Linzer Tarts, also known as "Linzertorte" in German, are a traditional Austrian pastry made with a buttery crust and a jam filling, usually made with raspberry or apricot jam.

Ingredients (6 Servings)

10 oz. all-purpose flour
6 oz. unsalted butter, room temperature
1 ½ oz. sugar
1 egg yolk
1 teaspoon vanilla extract
Pinch of salt
8 oz. raspberry or apricot jam
Powdered sugar, for dusting

Preparation

In a suitable-sized mixing bowl, combine the flour, butter, sugar, egg yolk, vanilla extract, and salt. Mix until a dough forms. Shape the prepared dough into a disk and wrap it in plastic wrap. Refrigerate for at least 30 minutes. At 350 degrees F, preheat your oven. Roll out the prepared dough on a lightly floured surface to about ⅛ inch thickness. Cut out the prepared dough into circles, using a round cookie cutter or a glass. Grease your muffin tin or line it with paper cups. Press the prepared dough circles into the cups. Spread about 1 teaspoon of jam in each cup, leaving a small border around the edge. Cut out small circles or shapes from the remaining dough to use as a lattice top. Place the prepared dough on top of the jam. Bake the tarts for 20-25 minutes or until the edges are golden brown. Remove the tarts from the oven and let them cool on a wire rack. Once cooled, dust them with powdered sugar.

Austrian Potato Plum Dumplings

Preparation time: 10 minutes
Cook time: 20 minutes
Nutrition facts (per serving): 233 Cal (11g fat, 7g protein, 2.1g fiber)

Potato plum dumplings, also known as "Kartoffelpflaumenknödel" in German, are a traditional Austrian dish made with boiled potatoes and dried plums.

Ingredients (6 Servings)

1 ¾ lb. potatoes

6 oz. dried plums

3 ½ oz. flour

1 egg

Salt, to taste

¼ cup breadcrumbs

¼ cup butter

Powdered sugar, for dusting

Preparation

Peel and boil the potatoes in salted water until they are tender. Mash the potatoes while they are still warm. Soak the dried plums in warm water for about 10 minutes, then drain and chop them. Mix together the mashed potatoes, flour, egg, and a pinch of salt. Add the chopped plums and knead the prepared dough until it comes together. Shape the prepared dough into dumplings, about the size of a tennis ball. Bring a suitable pot of water to a boil, and salt it generously. Roll the dumplings in breadcrumbs to coat them evenly. Carefully drop the dumplings into the boiling water, and cook them for about 20 minutes or until they float to the surface. Remove the dumplings from the pot and drain them. In a suitable pan, melt the butter and brown the dumplings on all sides. Serve the dumplings warm, dusted with powdered sugar.

Viennese Crescent Holiday Cookies

Preparation time: 10 minutes

Cook time: 15 minutes

Nutrition facts (per serving): 284 Cal (8g fat, 8g protein, 5g fiber)

Viennese crescent holiday cookies, also known as "Vanillekipferl" in German, are a traditional Austrian Christmas cookie made with ground almonds, butter, and vanilla.

Ingredients (6 Servings)

10 oz. ground almonds

6 oz. unsalted butter, at room temperature

3 ½ oz. powdered sugar

1 egg yolk

1 teaspoon vanilla extract

8 oz. all-purpose flour

Powdered sugar, for dusting

Preparation

In a suitable-sized bowl, combine the ground almonds, butter, powdered sugar, egg yolk, and vanilla extract. Mix until well combined. Slowly add the flour to the prepared mixture and knead the prepared dough until it comes together. Shape the prepared dough into a ball, wrap it in plastic wrap, and refrigerate for at least 30 minutes. At 350 degrees F, preheat your oven and line a baking sheet with parchment paper. Remove the prepared dough from the refrigerator and roll it into small crescent-shaped cookies. Place the cookies on the prepared baking sheet and bake for 12-15 minutes, or until they are golden brown. Remove these baked cookies from the oven and let them cool for a few minutes. Dust the cookies with powdered sugar before serving.

Salads

Austrian Potato Salad (Erdäpfelsalat)

Preparation time: 10 minutes
Cook time: 10 minutes
Nutrition facts (per serving): 291 Cal (3g fat, 8g protein, 1.9g fiber)

Austrian-style potato salad, also known as "Erdäpfelsalat" in German, is a traditional dish made with boiled potatoes, mayonnaise, and various herbs and spices.

Ingredients (4 Servings)

2 lbs. potatoes
¼ cup diced onion
¼ cup diced celery
¼ cup diced pickles
¼ cup chopped parsley
¼ cup chopped chives
½ cup mayonnaise
2 tablespoons white wine vinegar
Black pepper, to taste
Salt, to taste
Paprika powder, for garnish

Preparation

Peel and boil the potatoes in salted water until they are tender. Drain and let them cool. Cut the potatoes into bite-sized chunks and place them in a suitable-sized bowl. Add the diced onion, celery, pickles, parsley, and chives to the bowl. In a suitable-sized bowl, mix together the mayonnaise, white wine vinegar, salt, and pepper. Pour the mayonnaise mixture over the potato mixture and toss to combine. Cover this bowl and refrigerate it the salad for at least 30 minutes to allow the flavors to meld. Before serving, sprinkle some paprika powder over the top as garnish.

Austrian Cucumber Salad

Preparation time: 10 minutes
Nutrition facts (per serving): 118 Cal (4g fat, 4g protein, 6g fiber)

Austrian-style cucumber salad, also known as "Gurkensalat" in German, is a simple and refreshing dish made with fresh cucumbers and a simple vinegar-based dressing.

Ingredients (2 Servings)
2 large cucumbers, thinly sliced
¼ cup diced onion
¼ cup white wine vinegar
2 tablespoons extra-virgin olive oil
1 tablespoon granulated sugar
Black pepper, to taste
Salt, to taste
1 tablespoon chopped dill, for garnish

Preparation
Place the cucumber slices and diced onion in a suitable-sized bowl. In a suitable-sized bowl, mix together the white wine vinegar, olive oil, sugar, salt, and pepper. Pour the dressing over the cucumber mixture and toss to combine. Cover this bowl and refrigerate it the salad for at least 30 minutes to allow the flavors to meld. Before serving, sprinkle some chopped dill over the top as garnish.

Warm Potato Salad

Preparation time: 10 minutes
Cook time: 15 minutes
Nutrition facts (per serving): 303 Cal (8g fat, 8g protein, 2g fiber)

Warm Potato Salad is a side dish made with boiled potatoes that are diced or sliced, and then tossed with a warm dressing made with ingredients such as oil, vinegar, herbs, and spices. Some variations may also include ingredients such as bacon, onions, or eggs.

Ingredients (4 Servings)

2 lbs. small new potatoes
¼ cup white wine vinegar
2 tablespoons Dijon mustard
4 tablespoons olive oil
2 medium shallots, finely chopped
Salt, to taste
Black pepper, to taste
¼ cup chopped fresh parsley

Preparation

Cook the small potatoes in salted water until soft, for about 15 minutes. Drain and set aside. In a suitable-sized bowl, whisk together the vinegar, mustard, and olive oil. In a suitable-sized bowl, combine the warm potatoes, shallots, and dressing. Toss to combine and season with black pepper and salt to taste. Leave this salad to sit for 10 minutes to allow the flavors to meld. Before serving, sprinkle with chopped parsley. Enjoy!

Austrian Apple and Potato Salad

Preparation time: 10 minutes

Cook time: 10 minutes

Nutrition facts (per serving): 299 Cal (6g fat, 5g protein, 7g fiber)

Austrian-style apple and potato salad is a unique and delicious dish that combines the flavors of crisp apples and tender potatoes with a tangy dressing.

Ingredients (6 Servings)

2 lbs. potatoes

2 large apples

¼ cup diced onion

2 tablespoons apple cider vinegar

2 tablespoons extra-virgin olive oil

1 tablespoon granulated sugar

Black pepper, to taste

Salt, to taste

1 tablespoon chopped parsley, for garnish

Preparation

Peel and boil the potatoes in salted water until they are tender. Drain and let them cool. Cut the potatoes into bite-sized chunks and place them in a suitable-sized bowl. Cut the apples into small chunks, discarding the core and seeds. Add the apples to the bowl with the potatoes. Add the diced onion to the bowl. In a suitable-sized bowl, mix together the apple cider vinegar, olive oil, sugar, salt, and pepper. Pour the dressing over the apple and potato mixture and toss to combine. Cover this bowl and refrigerate it the salad for at least 30 minutes to allow the flavors to meld. Before serving, sprinkle some chopped parsley over the top as garnish.

Austrian Caesar Salad

Preparation time: 10 minutes
Nutrition facts (per serving): 277 Cal (3g fat, 4g protein, 8g fiber)

An Austrian Caesar Salad, also known as "Wiener Caesar Salad" in German, is a variation of the classic Caesar salad that's popular in Austria. It's typically made with different or additional ingredients compared to the original Caesar salad, and has a unique flavor profile.

Ingredients (2 Servings)

1 head of romaine lettuce, chopped
½ cup croutons
½ cup grated Parmesan cheese
2 anchovy fillets
2 cloves of garlic
1 egg yolk
1 tablespoon Dijon mustard
3 tablespoons red wine vinegar
½ cup extra-virgin olive oil
Black pepper, to taste
Salt, to taste

Preparation

In a suitable-sized bowl, combine the chopped lettuce, croutons, and grated Parmesan cheese. In a separate bowl, mash the anchovy fillets and garlic cloves together with a fork. Add the egg yolk, Dijon mustard, and red wine vinegar, and mix well. Slowly add olive oil, whisking constantly, until the dressing is emulsified. Season with black pepper and salt to taste. Pour the prepared dressing over the salad and toss to coat evenly. Divide the salad into individual servings and garnish with additional parmesan cheese and croutons if desired.

Austrian Green Bean Salad

Preparation time: 10 minutes
Cook time: 10 minutes
Nutrition facts (per serving): 250 Cal (1g fat, 6g protein, 1.7g fiber)

Austrian Green Bean Salad, also known as "Grüner Bohnensalat" in German, is a popular side dish in Austria. It's made with fresh green beans, and typically features a simple dressing made from oil, vinegar, and seasonings.

Ingredients (2 Servings)

1 lb. fresh green beans, trimmed

¼ cup diced red onion

¼ cup diced red bell pepper

2 tablespoons chopped fresh parsley

2 tablespoons white wine vinegar

2 tablespoons extra-virgin olive oil

1 teaspoon Dijon mustard

½ teaspoon sugar

Black pepper, to taste

Salt, to taste

Preparation

Bring a suitable pot of salted water to a boil. Add the trimmed green beans and cook until tender but still crisp, about 4-5 minutes. Drain and rinse the green beans under cold water to stop the cooking process. In a suitable-sized bowl, combine the cooked green beans, red onion, red bell pepper, and parsley. In a suitable-sized bowl, whisk together the white wine vinegar, olive oil, Dijon mustard, sugar, black pepper and salt to taste. Pour the dressing over the green bean mixture, and toss to coat evenly. Cover this bowl and refrigerate it for at least 30 minutes to allow the flavors to meld. Before serving, taste and adjust the seasoning as needed.

Tomatensalat

Preparation time: 10 minutes
Nutrition facts (per serving): 144 Cal (3g fat, 5g protein, 8g fiber)

Tomatensalat, also known as "Tomato Salad" in English, is a simple and refreshing dish that's popular in Austria.

Ingredients (4 Servings)

2 lbs. ripe tomatoes, cored and diced

¼ cup diced red onion

2 tablespoons chopped fresh parsley

2 tablespoons red wine vinegar

2 tablespoons extra-virgin olive oil

1 teaspoon Dijon mustard

Black pepper, to taste

Salt, to taste

Preparation

In a suitable-sized bowl, combine the diced tomatoes, red onion, and parsley. In a suitable-sized bowl, whisk together the red wine vinegar, olive oil, Dijon mustard, black pepper and salt to taste. Add the prepared dressing over the tomato mixture, and toss to coat evenly. Cover this bowl and refrigerate it for at least 30 minutes to allow the flavors to meld. Before serving, taste and adjust the seasoning as needed.

Warm Endive Salad

Preparation time: 10 minutes
Cook time: 12 minutes
Nutrition facts (per serving): 255 Cal (3g fat, 4g protein, 7g fiber)

Warm Endive Salad is a dish that features endive leaves that are wilted or gently sautéed and then combined with other ingredients to create a warm and flavorful salad. Endive is a type of lettuce that has a slightly bitter flavor and a crisp, crunchy texture.

Ingredients (4 Servings)
4 Belgian endives, chopped
4 oz. bacon, diced
2 tablespoons white wine vinegar
1 tablespoon Dijon mustard
Black pepper, to taste
Salt, to taste
¼ cup olive oil
2 tablespoons chopped fresh parsley

Preparation
In a suitable skillet, cook the bacon over medium heat until crispy. Remove the bacon from the skillet and set aside. In a suitable-sized bowl, whisk together the white wine vinegar, Dijon mustard, salt, pepper, and olive oil. Add the chopped endives to the skillet and pour the dressing over the top. Toss to combine and cook until the endives are wilted and heated through, about 5 minutes. Stir in the bacon and parsley. Serve the warm endive salad as a side dish. Enjoy!

Coachman's Salad

Preparation time: 10 minutes
Nutrition facts (per serving): 290 Cal (7g fat, 4g protein, 5g fiber)

Coachman's Salad, also known as "Kutschker Salat" in German, is a traditional Austrian salad that's typically made with potatoes, cucumbers, and onions.

Ingredients (4 Servings)
2 large potatoes, peeled and diced
1 large cucumber, diced
1 small red onion, diced
2 tablespoons chopped fresh parsley
2 tablespoons red wine vinegar
2 tablespoons extra-virgin olive oil
1 teaspoon Dijon mustard
Black pepper, to taste
Salt, to taste

Preparation
In a suitable pot of boiling water, cook the potatoes until tender, about 8-10 minutes. Drain and let cool. In a suitable-sized bowl, combine the cooked potatoes, diced cucumber, red onion, and parsley. In a suitable-sized bowl, whisk together the red wine vinegar, olive oil, Dijon mustard, salt, and pepper to taste. Pour the dressing over the salad mixture and toss to coat evenly. Cover this bowl and refrigerate it for at least 30 minutes to allow the flavors to meld. Before serving, taste and adjust the seasoning as needed.

Austrian Pear Salad with Raspberry Vinaigrette

Preparation time: 10 minutes
Nutrition facts (per serving): 275 Cal (4g fat, 7g protein, 6g fiber)

Austrian Pear Salad with Raspberry Vinaigrette is a delicious and refreshing salad that combines the sweet taste of pears with the tangy flavor of raspberries.

Ingredients (4 Servings)
4 cups mixed salad greens
2 ripe pears, cored and sliced
¼ cup fresh raspberries
2 tablespoons chopped fresh parsley
2 tablespoons chopped fresh mint
2 tablespoons chopped toasted pecans
2 tablespoons fresh lemon juice
2 tablespoons honey
1 tablespoon raspberry vinegar
¼ cup extra-virgin olive oil
Black pepper, to taste
Salt, to taste

Preparation
In a suitable-sized bowl, combine the salad greens, pears, raspberries, parsley, mint, and pecans. In another bowl, whisk the lemon juice, honey, raspberry vinegar, olive oil, black pepper and salt. Add the prepared dressing over the salad and toss to coat evenly. Serve immediately.

Potato Salad with Chipotle Peppers

Preparation time: 10 minutes
Cook time: 15 minutes
Nutrition facts (per serving): 321 Cal (7g fat, 4g protein, 2.4g fiber)

Potato salad with chipotle peppers is a delicious and spicy variation of traditional potato salad.

Ingredients (4 Servings)
2 lbs. Yukon gold potatoes, peeled and diced
¾ cup mayonnaise
¼ cup sour cream
2 tablespoons Dijon mustard
2 tablespoons fresh lemon juice
2 cloves garlic, minced
1 teaspoon honey
½ teaspoon smoked paprika
¼ teaspoon salt
¼ teaspoon black pepper
¼ cup chopped fresh cilantro
2 chipotle peppers in adobo sauce, minced
¼ cup green onions, chopped

Preparation
Bring a suitable pot of salted water to a boil. Add the potatoes and cook for 12-15 minutes or until tender. Drain and let cool. In a suitable-sized bowl, combine the mayonnaise, sour cream, Dijon mustard, lemon juice,

garlic, honey, smoked paprika, salt, and pepper. Stir in the cilantro, chipotle peppers, and green onions. Add the cooled potatoes to the dressing and toss to coat evenly. Refrigerate for at least 30 minutes to allow the flavors to meld. Serve chilled and enjoy!

Soups and Stews

Alt-Wiener Suppenhuhn

Preparation time: 10 minutes
Cook time: 1 hour 20 minutes
Nutrition facts (per serving): 338 Cal (6g fat, 36g protein, 5g fiber)

Alt-Wiener Suppenhuhn, also known as Old Vienna Soup Chicken, is a traditional Austrian dish that's typically served in a clear broth with various vegetables and dumplings.

Ingredients (8 Servings)
1 whole chicken
1 onion, peeled and quartered
2 carrots, peeled and cut into chunks
2 celery stalks, cut into chunks
2 cloves of garlic, peeled and crushed
1 bay leaf
2 tablespoons parsley, chopped
2 tablespoons chives, chopped
Black pepper, to taste
Salt, to taste
2 cups flour
2 eggs
½ cup water
2 tablespoons parsley, chopped

Preparation

In a suitable pot, combine the chicken, onion, carrots, celery, garlic, bay leaf, parsley, and chives. Cover with cold water and cook to a boil. Reduce its heat and cook on a simmer for about 1 hour or until the chicken is cooked through. Remove the cooked chicken from the pot and let it cool. Remove its meat from the bones and shred it into small pieces. In another separate bowl, mix together the flour, eggs, water, and parsley until a smooth dough forms. Heat the soup back to a boil and drop spoonfuls of the prepared dough into the pot. Cook the dumplings for about 10 minutes or until they are cooked through. Add the shredded chicken meat back into the pot and season the soup with black pepper and salt to taste. Simmer for an additional 10 minutes to heat through. Serve in bowls and enjoy.

Fritatten Soupe

Preparation time: 10 minutes
Cook time: 20 minutes
Nutrition facts (per serving): 378 Cal (14g fat, 4g protein, 3g fiber)

Fritatten Suppe is a traditional Austrian soup made with thin egg noodle fritters (called "Fritatten") in a clear broth. It can also include ingredients such as vegetables, meat, or herbs.

Ingredients (6 Servings)

4 medium-sized potatoes

2 medium-sized carrots

2 medium-sized onions

1 small head of celery

1 cup of diced ham

3 tablespoons of flour

3 tablespoons of butter

4 cups of chicken broth

Black pepper, to taste

Salt, to taste

2 cups of heavy cream

Fresh parsley, to garnish

Preparation

Dice the potatoes, carrots, onions, and celery into small pieces. In a suitable pot, melt the butter and add the diced vegetables. Cook for 5 minutes until softened. Add the dry flour and cook for 2 minutes, stirring continuously. Pour in the chicken broth and cook to a boil. Reduce heat and cook on a simmer for 15 minutes. Add the diced ham and season with black pepper and salt. Pour in the heavy cream and stir to combine. Simmer for 5 more minutes, then remove from heat. Serve hot, garnished with fresh parsley. Enjoy!

Traditional Austrian Soup (Klachelsuppe)

Preparation time: 10 minutes
Cook time: 25 minutes
Nutrition facts (per serving): 394 Cal (11g fat, 23g protein, 1.4g fiber)

Klachelsuppe is a traditional Austrian soup made with small dumplings called Klöße, which are similar to Italian gnocchi.

Ingredients (8 Servings)

2 cups flour

2 eggs

½ cup water

2 tablespoons parsley, chopped

Black pepper, to taste

Salt, to taste

6 cups chicken or beef broth

2 cups diced cooked beef or pork

2 tablespoons butter

2 tablespoons flour

1 cup milk

2 tablespoons sour cream

1 tablespoon chopped chives

Preparation

In a suitable-sized bowl, mix together the flour, eggs, water, and parsley until a smooth dough forms. Season with a pinch of black pepper and salt. Cook the broth to a boil in a suitable pot. Using a spoon, drop small dumplings of dough into the boiling broth. Cook the dumplings for about 10 minutes or until they are cooked through. Remove the dumplings from the broth with a slotted spoon and set them aside. If using, add the diced cooked beef or pork to the broth and cook on a simmer for a few minutes to heat through. In a separate suitable pan, melt the butter over medium heat. Whisk in the flour to make a roux. Slowly add the milk, whisking constantly to prevent lumps. Cook for a few minutes, or until the prepared mixture thickens. Stir the roux into the broth and bring the soup to a simmer. Once the soup has thickened, add the cooked dumplings, sour cream, and chopped chives. Season the soup with black pepper and salt to taste. Serve in bowls and enjoy!

Austrian Pumpkin Soup (Kürbis Suppe)

Preparation time: 10 minutes
Cook time: 45 minutes
Nutrition facts (per serving): 327 Cal (17g fat, 15g protein, 2g fiber)

Kürbis Suppe, also known as pumpkin soup, is a traditional and comforting dish in Austria. It's often seasoned with spices such as cinnamon, nutmeg, and ginger and can be served hot or cold. The pumpkin is usually cooked and blended with broth or cream to make a smooth and creamy soup.

Ingredients (4 Servings)

1 small pumpkin, peeled and diced
1 onion, chopped
2 cloves of garlic, minced
4 cups chicken or vegetable broth
1 cup heavy cream
Black pepper and salt, to taste
2 tablespoons butter
2 tablespoons flour
1 cup milk
2 tablespoons sour cream
1 tablespoon chopped chives

Preparation

In a suitable pot, melt the butter over medium heat. Add the chopped onion and garlic and sauté until softened. Add the diced pumpkin and broth to the pot. Bring the prepared mixture to a boil, then reduce heat to low and let it simmer for 20-25 minutes or until the pumpkin is very tender. Once the pumpkin is cooked, use an immersion blender or a regular blender to puree the soup until it is smooth. Return the soup to the pot and add the cream, salt, and pepper. Bring the soup to a simmer. In a separate suitable pan, melt the butter over medium heat. Whisk in the flour to make a roux. Slowly add the milk, whisking constantly to prevent lumps. Cook for a few minutes, or until the prepared mixture thickens. Stir the roux into the soup and bring it to a simmer. Once the soup has thickened, add the sour cream and chopped chives. Season the soup with additional black pepper and salt, to taste. Serve in bowls and enjoy!

Speckknödelsuppe

Preparation time: 10 minutes
Cook time: 25 minutes
Nutrition facts (per serving): 391 Cal (7g fat, 31g protein, 4g fiber)

Speckknödelsuppe is a traditional Austrian soup made with dumplings made from bread or potatoes and bacon or ham. The dumplings are typically boiled in a flavorful broth made from beef or chicken stock and served with slices of the bacon or ham. Some variations may also include additional ingredients such as herbs, onions, or carrots to add flavor to the soup.

Ingredients (4 Servings)
1 lb. bacon, diced
1 onion, chopped
2 cloves of garlic, minced
4 cups chicken or beef broth
2 cups water
Black pepper, to taste
Salt, to taste
2 cups flour
4 eggs
¼ cup milk
2 tablespoons parsley, chopped

Preparation

In a suitable pot, sauté the bacon over medium heat until crispy. Remove this cooked bacon from the pot and set it aside. In the same pot, add the onion and garlic and sauté until softened. Add the broth and water to the pot, and bring the prepared mixture to a boil. Reduce its heat to low and let it simmer. In a suitable-sized bowl, combine the flour, eggs, milk, parsley, and a pinch of black pepper and salt. Mix well until a dough forms. Roll the prepared dough into small balls, about the size of a golf ball. Carefully drop the dumplings into the simmering broth. Cover this pot and let it simmer for about 10-15 minutes, or until the dumplings are cooked through. Add the reserved bacon to the soup, and season it with additional black pepper and salt, to taste. Serve in bowls and enjoy!

Austrian Beef Soup (Rindsuppe)

Preparation time: 10 minutes
Cook time: 2 hours 30 minutes
Nutrition facts (per serving): 401 Cal (20g fat, 29g protein, 2.4g fiber)

Rindsuppe is a traditional Austrian beef soup made with a beef broth base and various vegetables and meats.

Ingredients (2 Servings)
1 lb. beef shank or marrow bones
2 onions, chopped
2 carrots, chopped
2 celery stalks, chopped
2 cloves of garlic, minced
2 bay leaves
1 teaspoon thyme
Black pepper, to taste
Salt, to taste
2 cups beef broth
2 cups water
2 cups diced potatoes
1 cup diced carrots
1 cup diced celery
1 cup diced onion
2 tablespoons parsley, chopped

Preparation

In a suitable pot, brown the beef shank or marrow bones over medium heat. Remove the meat and set it aside. In the same pot, add the onions, carrots, and celery and sauté until softened. Add the garlic, bay leaves, thyme, black pepper and salt and sauté for 1 more minute. Add the beef broth, water and browned beef shank or marrow bones to the pot and bring the prepared mixture to a boil. Reduce its heat to low and let it simmer for 2 hours. Remove the beef shank or marrow bones from the pot and let them cool. Remove its meat from the bones and shred it. Add the shredded meat, diced potatoes, carrots, celery, and onion to the pot and let it simmer for another 30 minutes or until the vegetables are tender. Season it with additional black pepper and salt, to taste. Serve in bowls and garnish with chopped parsley.

Austrian Garlic Soup with Croutons

Preparation time: 10 minutes

Cook time: 10 minutes

Nutrition facts (per serving): 208 Cal (10g fat, 25g protein, 3g fiber)

The soup is typically made by sautéing garlic in butter or oil, then adding broth and bread to the pan to make a thick and creamy soup. Croutons, which are small pieces of toasted bread, are often added to the soup for texture and flavor. The soup is typically seasoned with salt, pepper, and herbs such as parsley or chives, and is served hot as a starter or main course.

Ingredients (4 Servings)

2 cups chicken or vegetable broth

2 cups water

1 head of garlic, cloves peeled and minced

2 tablespoons butter

2 tablespoons flour

1 cup heavy cream

Black pepper, to taste

Salt, to taste

4 slices of bread, cut into small cubes

2 tablespoons olive oil

Preparation

In a suitable pot, bring the broth and water to a boil. Add the garlic to the pot and Reduce its heat to a simmer. In a separate pan, melt the butter over medium heat. Add the flour and stir to combine, cooking for 1-2 minutes. Slowly pour the butter and flour mixture into the pot with the broth and garlic. Stir in the cream and season with black pepper and salt to taste. In another suitable pan, heat the olive oil over medium heat. Add the bread cubes and toss to coat in the oil. Fry the bread cubes until they are golden brown and crispy. Divide the cooked soup into bowls and top with the croutons before serving.

Austrian Clear Soup with Semolina Dumplings

Preparation time: 10 minutes

Cook time: 17 minutes

Nutrition facts (per serving): 240 Cal (23g fat, 25g protein, 2.4g fiber)

Austrian clear soup with semolina dumplings is a traditional soup dish from Austria that is made with a clear broth, usually chicken or beef, and semolina dumplings. The dumplings are made from a mixture of semolina flour, eggs, and milk and are added to the broth to cook.

Ingredients (4 Servings)

2 quarts chicken or vegetable broth

2 cups water

1 onion, finely chopped

2 carrots, finely chopped

2 celery stalks, finely chopped

Black pepper, to taste

Salt, to taste

½ cup semolina flour

2 eggs, lightly beaten

2 tablespoons parsley, finely chopped

Preparation

In a suitable pot, bring the broth and water to a boil. Add the finely chopped onion, carrots, and celery to the pot and Reduce its heat to a simmer. Season the soup with black pepper and salt to taste. In a separate bowl, mix the semolina flour, eggs, and parsley. Using a teaspoon, drop small dumplings into the simmering soup. Cook the dumplings for 5-7 minutes, or until they're cooked through. Ladle the soup into bowls and serve.

Austrian Style Cold Vegetable Soup

Preparation time: 10 minutes

Cook time: 25 minutes

Nutrition facts (per serving): 307 Cal (14g fat, 18g protein, 1.3g fiber)

Austrian-style cold vegetable soup is a chilled soup that is traditionally made with a variety of raw or cooked vegetables, such as cucumbers, carrots, bell peppers, and tomatoes, and is typically seasoned with herbs such as dill, parsley, and chives. The soup is often served cold, which makes it a refreshing dish for summer.

Ingredients (4 Servings)

2 cups chicken broth

2 cups water

2 cups diced potatoes

1 cup diced carrots

1 cup diced celery

1 cup diced cucumber

1 cup diced green bell pepper

1 cup diced tomatoes

2 cups diced onions

1 cup sour cream

2 tablespoons chopped dill

Black pepper, to taste

Salt, to taste

Preparation

In a suitable pot, bring the broth and water to a boil. Add the diced potatoes, carrots, celery, cucumber, bell pepper and tomatoes, and onions. Reduce its heat to low and cook on a simmer for 10-15 minutes, or until the vegetables are tender. Remove this pot from the heat and let the soup cool. Once the soup is cool, transfer it to a blender and blend until smooth. Stir in the sour cream and chopped dill. Season the soup with black pepper and salt to taste. Chill the soup in the refrigerator for at least 2 hours. Serve the soup chilled, garnished with additional dill, if desired.

Austrian Fish Soup

Preparation time: 10 minutes

Cook time: 17 minutes

Nutrition facts (per serving): 412 Cal (22g fat, 29g protein, 4g fiber)

Austrian fish soup is a traditional soup dish made with fish, usually whitefish, as the main ingredient. The soup is typically made with a fish or seafood stock, and may include additional ingredients such as onions, celery, carrots, potatoes, and herbs such as parsley and dill. The fish is usually poached in the broth and then flaked into the soup.

Ingredients (4 Servings)

2 quarts fish stock or fish broth

2 cups water

1 onion, finely chopped

2 cloves of garlic, minced

2 carrots, sliced

2 celery stalks, sliced

2 cups diced tomatoes

1 cup white wine

2 cups mixed fish fillets (cod, haddock, and salmon)

2 cups heavy cream

2 tablespoons parsley, chopped

Black pepper, to taste

Salt, to taste

Preparation

In a suitable pot, bring the fish stock or fish broth and water to a boil. Add the onion, garlic, carrots, celery, and tomatoes to the pot. Reduce its heat to a simmer and add the white wine. Add the fish fillets to the pot and cook for 5-7 minutes, or until the fish is cooked through. Stir in the heavy cream and chopped parsley. Season the soup with black pepper and salt to taste. Ladle the soup into bowls and serve.

Goulash Soup
(Gulaschsuppe)

Preparation time: 10 minutes
Cook time: 35 minutes
Nutrition facts (pe serving): 393 Cal (20g fat, 32g protein, 1.6g fiber)

Gulaschsuppe is a soup made with beef, paprika, onions, and potatoes as the main ingredients. The beef is typically diced or sliced and browned in a pan, then simmered with the onions and paprika in a beef or chicken broth to make a rich and flavorful soup. Potatoes are added to the soup to thicken it and to provide a more substantial texture.

Ingredients (4 Servings)
1 lb. beef (stewing beef), cut into small cubes
1 onion, chopped
2 cloves of garlic, minced
2 tablespoons vegetable oil
2 tablespoons paprika powder
1 teaspoon caraway seeds
1 teaspoon salt
¼ teaspoon black pepper
1 cup beef broth
1 cup water
1 potato, peeled and diced
1 carrot, peeled and diced
1 cup diced tomatoes
1 cup sour cream, optional

Preparation

In a suitable pot or Dutch oven, heat the oil over medium-high heat. Place the beef and sear until browned on all sides. Toss in the onion and garlic and cook until softened. Stir in the paprika, caraway seeds, salt, and pepper, and cook for 1 minute. Add the beef broth and water, and cook to a boil. Reduce its heat to low, and add the potato, carrot, and tomatoes. Cook on a simmer for 30 minutes until the vegetables are tender. Stir in the sour cream (if using) and heat through. Serve hot.

Austrian Beef Stew (Rindsgulasch)

Preparation time: 10 minutes
Cook time: 1 hour 20 minutes
Nutrition facts (per serving): 428 Cal (14g fat, 35g protein, 2g fiber)

Rindsgulasch is a dish made with beef, onions, paprika, and a variety of spices. The beef is typically diced or sliced and browned in a pan, then simmered with the onions and paprika in a beef or chicken broth to make a rich and flavorful stew.

Ingredients (4 Servings)
2 lb. beef (stewing beef), cut into small cubes
2 onions, chopped
2 cloves of garlic, minced
2 tablespoons vegetable oil
2 tablespoons paprika powder
1 teaspoon caraway seeds
1 teaspoon salt
¼ teaspoon black pepper
1 cup beef broth
1 cup red wine
1 bay leaf
2 tablespoons tomato paste
2 tablespoons flour
1 cup sour cream

Preparation

In a suitable pot or Dutch oven, heat the oil over medium-high heat. Place the beef and cook until browned on all sides. Add the onions and garlic and cook until softened. Stir in the paprika, caraway seeds, salt, and pepper, and cook for 1 minute. Pour in the beef broth, red wine, and add the bay leaf. Cook to a boil, Reduce its heat and let it simmer for about 1 hour or until the meat is tender. In a suitable-sized bowl, mix together the tomato paste and flour until smooth. Stir this mixture into the stew and cook to a boil, then Reduce its heat and let it simmer for another 15 minutes. Discard the bay leaf and stir in the sour cream. Heat through, but do not boil. Serve hot.

Austrian Potato Goulash

Preparation time: 10 minutes
Cook time: 35 minutes
Nutrition facts (per serving): 410 Cal (31g fat, 11g protein, 2g fiber)

Potato goulash is a traditional Central European dish made with potatoes, onions, and paprika as the main ingredients. The dish is typically made by sautéing onions in a pan, then adding diced potatoes, paprika, and broth or water to make a hearty and flavorful stew.

Ingredients (4 Servings)
2 lb. potatoes, peeled and diced
2 cups beef broth
1 onion, chopped
2 cloves of garlic, minced
2 tablespoons vegetable oil
2 tablespoons paprika powder
1 teaspoon caraway seeds
1 teaspoon salt
¼ teaspoon black pepper
1 cup sour cream

Preparation
In a suitable pot or Dutch oven, heat the oil over medium-high heat. Toss in the onion and garlic and cook until softened. Stir in the paprika, caraway seeds, salt, and pepper, and cook for 1 minute. Add the potatoes and beef broth, cook to a boil. Reduce its heat to low, and let it simmer

for about 20-25 minutes or until the potatoes are tender. Remove from heat and let it cool for a few minutes. Add the sour cream and heat through, but do not boil. Serve hot.

Main Dishes

Cabbie Goulash (Fiakergulasch)

Preparation time: 10 minutes
Cook time: 1 hour 10 minutes
Nutrition facts (per serving): 406 Cal (24g fat, 36g protein, 4g fiber)

Fiakergulasch, also known as "Cabbie's Goulash," is a traditional Austrian dish that's said to have originated from the goulash that was served to the horse-drawn carriage drivers, or "Fiakers," in Vienna.

Ingredients (4 Servings)

2 lb. beef (stewing beef), cut into small cubes
2 onions, chopped
2 cloves of garlic, minced
2 tablespoons vegetable oil
2 tablespoons paprika powder
1 teaspoon caraway seeds
1 teaspoon salt
¼ teaspoon black pepper
1 cup beef broth
1 cup red wine
1 bay leaf
2 tablespoons tomato paste
2 tablespoons flour
½ cup chopped fresh parsley

Preparation

In a suitable pot or Dutch oven, heat the oil over medium-high heat. Sear the beef and cook until browned on all sides. Add the onions and garlic and cook until softened. Stir in the paprika, caraway seeds, salt, and pepper, and cook for 1 minute. Pour in the beef broth, red wine, and add the bay leaf. Cook to a boil, Reduce its heat and let it simmer for about 1 hour or until the meat is tender. In a suitable-sized bowl, mix together the tomato paste and flour until smooth. Stir this mixture into the stew and cook to a boil, then Reduce its heat and let it simmer for another 15 minutes. Discard the bay leaf and stir in the chopped parsley. Serve hot.

Austrian Martinigans

Preparation time: 10 minutes
Cook time: 2 hours 45 minutes
Nutrition facts (per serving): 413 Cal (23g fat, 41g protein, 3g fiber)

Martini Gans, also known as Martinsgans, is a traditional Austrian dish typically served around St. Martin's Day (Martinstag) which is celebrated on November 11th. It's a roasted goose dish that is often served with red cabbage and knödel (dumplings) or bread dumplings.

Ingredients (16 Servings)
1 (8-10 lb.) goose
Black pepper and salt, to taste
2 onions, chopped
2 cloves of garlic, minced
2 cups red wine
2 cups chicken or beef broth
2 tablespoons butter
2 tablespoons flour
1 cup sour cream
2 cups red cabbage, cooked
2 cups bread dumplings

Preparation
At 375 degrees F, preheat your oven. Season the goose with black pepper and salt. In a suitable pot or Dutch oven, sauté the onions and garlic in the butter until softened. Add the red wine and broth and cook to a boil.

Place the goose on a rack in a roasting pan and pour the hot liquid over it. Roast in the oven for about 2 ½ hours or until the internal temperature of the goose reaches 165°F (74°C). Remove the goose from the roasting pan and let it rest for 10-15 minutes. Strain the liquid from the roasting pan and return it to the pot. In a suitable-sized bowl, mix together the flour and sour cream until smooth. Slowly stir this mixture into the strained liquid and bring it to a boil. Reduce its heat and let it simmer for about 15 minutes or until thickened. Carve the goose and serve it with the gravy, red cabbage, and bread dumplings.

Bauernschmaus

Preparation time: 10 minutes
Cook time: 1 hour 30 minutes
Nutrition facts (per serving): 377 Cal (10g fat, 14g protein, 4g fiber)

Bauernschmaus, also known as "Farmers' feast," is a traditional Austrian dish that's a hearty and comforting combination of different meats, sausages, and vegetables. It's typically served with a gravy or sauce, and is often accompanied by bread dumplings or potato dumplings.

Ingredients (6 Servings)
2 lb. pork shoulder or beef stew meat, cut into bite-size chunks
2 lb. smoked pork belly or bacon, cut into bite-size chunks
2 lb. smoked sausages, sliced
2 onions, chopped
2 cloves of garlic, minced
2 tablespoons vegetable oil
2 tablespoons paprika powder
1 teaspoon caraway seeds
1 teaspoon salt
¼ teaspoon black pepper
1 cup beef or pork broth
1 cup red or white wine
2 cups sauerkraut, rinsed and drained
2 cups sliced potatoes
1 cup flour
1 cup sour cream

Preparation

In a suitable pot or Dutch oven, heat the oil over medium-high heat. Add the pork shoulder or beef, smoked pork belly or bacon, sausages, onions, and garlic. Cook until browned on all sides. Stir in the paprika, caraway seeds, salt, and pepper, and cook for 1 minute. Pour in the broth, red or white wine, sauerkraut, and sliced potatoes. Cook to a boil, Reduce its heat and let it simmer for about 1 hour or until the meats are tender. In a suitable-sized bowl, mix together the flour and sour cream until smooth. Slowly stir this mixture into the stew and cook to a boil, then Reduce its heat and let it simmer for another 15 minutes. Serve hot with bread dumplings or potato dumplings.

Cabbage Noodles (Krautfleckerl)

Preparation time: 10 minutes
Cook time: 35 minutes
Nutrition facts (per serving): 319 Cal (8g fat, 7g protein, 1.4g fiber)

Krautfleckerl, also known as "Cabbage noodles," is a traditional Austrian dish that combines sauerkraut with a type of pasta called "fleckerl." It's a hearty and delicious dish that's often served as a main course.

Ingredients (6 Servings)

1 lb. sauerkraut, rinsed and drained
1 onion, finely chopped
2 cloves of garlic, minced
2 tablespoons butter
1 cup chicken or beef broth
½ cup sour cream
¼ cup flour
Black pepper, to taste
Salt, to taste
1 lb. pasta or egg noodles
2 tablespoons parsley, chopped

Preparation

In a suitable pot or Dutch oven, sauté the onion and garlic in the butter until softened. Add the sauerkraut and stir well. Pour in the broth, cook to a boil, reduce the heat, and let it simmer for about 20 minutes. In a suitable-sized bowl, mix together the sour cream and flour until smooth. Slowly stir this mixture into the sauerkraut and cook to a boil, then Reduce its heat and let it simmer for another 10 minutes. Season with black pepper and salt to taste. Cook the Fleckerl pasta or egg noodles according to package instructions until al dente. Drain the cooked pasta and add it to the sauerkraut mixture. Stir well, heat through and serve hot, garnished with chopped parsley.

Cheese Noodles
(Kasnudeln)

Preparation time: 10 minutes
Cook time: 15 minutes
Nutrition facts (per serving): 302 Cal (4g fat, 38g protein, 1g fiber)

Kasnudeln, also known as "cheese noodles," is a traditional Austrian dish that combines a type of fresh pasta dough filled with a mixture of farmer's cheese and herbs. They're typically served with a butter-based sauce and garnished with chives.

Ingredients (4 Servings)
1 lb. of fresh pasta dough
1 cup farmer's cheese
¼ cup chopped chives
¼ cup chopped parsley
1 egg yolk
1 cup butter
¼ cup flour
2 cups milk
Black pepper, to taste
Salt, to taste
Chives, chopped, for garnish

Preparation
In a suitable-sized bowl, mix together the farmer's cheese, chives, parsley, egg yolk, black pepper and salt. Roll out the pasta dough on a lightly

floured surface to about ⅛ inch thickness. Using a spoon, place small mounds of the cheese mixture on half of the prepared dough, leaving about 1 inch of space between each mound. Fold the other half of the prepared dough over the cheese mixture, then press the edges together to seal. Cut the prepared dough into small rectangles. Bring a suitable pot of salted water to a boil and add the kasnudeln. Cook for about 3-5 minutes, or until they float to the surface. Drain the kasnudeln, and keep them warm. In another separate saucepan, melt the butter over medium heat. Stir in the dry flour and cook for about 2 minutes. Slowly whisk in the milk and cook to a boil. Reduce its heat and let it simmer for about 5 minutes, or until thickened. Season the sauce with black pepper and salt to taste. Serve the kasnudeln with the sauce, garnished with chopped chives.

Kasnocken

Preparation time: 10 minutes

Cook time: 15 minutes

Nutrition facts (per serving): 297 Cal (5g fat, 41g protein, 1.2g fiber)

Kasnocken, also known as "cheese gnocchi," is a traditional Austrian dish that combines small dumplings made of a mixture of farmer's cheese and flour. They're typically served with a butter-based sauce and garnished with chives.

Ingredients (4 Servings)

1 lb. of farmer's cheese

½ cup all-purpose flour

2 eggs

2 tablespoons chopped chives

Black pepper, to taste

Salt, to taste

1 cup butter

¼ cup flour

2 cups milk

Chives, chopped for garnish

Preparation

In a suitable-sized bowl, mix together the farmer's cheese, flour, eggs, chives, black pepper and salt until well combined. Shape the prepared mixture into small dumplings, about the size of a large grape. Bring a suitable pot of salted water to a boil. Gently add the dumplings to the boiling water and cook for about 3-5 minutes, or until they float to the surface. Drain the dumplings and keep them warm. In another saucepan, melt the butter over medium heat. Stir in the dry flour and cook for about 2 minutes. Slowly whisk in the milk and cook to a boil. Reduce its heat and let it simmer for about 5 minutes, or until thickened. Season the sauce with black pepper and salt to taste. Serve the kasnocken with the sauce, garnished with chopped chives.

Veal Meatloaf (Bruckfleisch)

Preparation time: 10 minutes
Cook time: 60 minutes
Nutrition facts (per serving): 298 Cal (11g fat, 23g protein, 4g fiber)

Here's a traditional dish from Austria that's made from beef or veal. It's a type of meatloaf that's typically flavored with herbs and spices, and is often served with a gravy or sauce.

Ingredients (2 Servings)

1 lb. beef or veal
1 onion, finely chopped
2 cloves of garlic, minced
1 egg
¼ cup breadcrumbs
¼ cup milk
1 teaspoon salt
½ teaspoon black pepper
¼ teaspoon nutmeg
2 tablespoons butter
1 cup beef broth
1 tablespoon cornstarch
2 tablespoons chopped parsley, optional

Preparation

At 350 degrees F, preheat your oven. In a suitable-sized mixing bowl, combine the beef or veal, onion, garlic, egg, breadcrumbs, milk, salt, pepper, and nutmeg. Mix well. Form the prepared mixture into a loaf shape and place it in a baking dish. Melt the butter in a suitable saucepan and brush it over the meatloaf. Bake the meatloaf in the preheated oven for about 1 hour, or until cooked through. While your meatloaf is cooking, make the gravy by combining the beef broth and cornstarch in a suitable saucepan. Cook to a boil and stir until thickened. Remove this baked meatloaf from the oven and let it rest for 10 minutes before slicing. Serve the Bruckfleisch with the gravy and chopped parsley, if desired.

Poppy Seed Noodles
(Mohnnudeln)

Preparation time: 10 minutes
Cook time: 12 minutes
Nutrition facts (per serving): 411 Cal (7g fat, 41g protein, 1.2g fiber)

Mohnnudeln, also known as "poppy seed noodles," is a traditional Austrian dish that combines a type of fresh pasta dough filled with a mixture of poppy seeds, sugar and milk. They're typically served with a butter-based sauce and garnished with sugar.

Ingredients (4 Servings)

1 lb. of fresh pasta dough
½ cup poppy seeds
¼ cup sugar
½ cup milk
1 egg yolk
Black pepper, to taste
Salt, to taste
1 cup butter
¼ cup flour
2 cups milk
Powdered sugar, for garnish

Preparation

In a suitable saucepan, heat the milk and sugar together until sugar has dissolved. Remove from heat and stir in the poppy seeds and let the prepared mixture cool. Roll out the pasta dough on a lightly floured surface to about ⅛ inch thickness. Place small mounds of the poppy seed mixture on half of the prepared dough, leaving about 1 inch of space between each mound. Fold the other half of the prepared dough over the poppy seed mixture, then press the edges together to seal. Cut the prepared dough into small rectangles. Bring a suitable pot of salted water to a boil and add the Mohnnudeln. Cook for about 3-5 minutes, or until they float to the surface. Drain the Mohnnudeln, and keep them warm. In a suitable saucepan, melt the butter over medium heat. Stir in the dry flour and cook for about 2 minutes. Slowly whisk in the milk and cook to a boil. Reduce its heat and let it simmer for about 5 minutes, or until thickened. Season the sauce with black pepper and salt to taste. Serve the Mohnnudeln with the sauce, garnished with powdered sugar.

Mezzelune

Preparation time: 10 minutes

Cook time: 5 minutes

Nutrition facts (per serving): 260 Cal (4g fat, 30g protein, 3g fiber)

It's also known as "half-moon" or "crescent-shaped" pasta, a traditional Italian dish made from a type of filled pasta. They're filled with a mixture of meat, cheese, or vegetables, and are usually served in a sauce or with melted butter.

Ingredients (2 Servings)

1 lb. of fresh pasta dough

1 cup of ricotta cheese

½ cup of grated Parmesan cheese

¼ cup of chopped fresh parsley

1 egg yolk

Black pepper, to taste

Salt, to taste

1 cup of your favorite pasta sauce

Parmesan cheese, for garnish

Preparation

In a suitable-sized mixing bowl, mix together the ricotta cheese, Parmesan cheese, parsley, egg yolk, black pepper and salt. Roll out the pasta dough on a lightly floured surface to about ⅛ inch thickness. Cut the pasta dough into circles using a round cookie cutter or a glass. Place a small amount of the cheese mixture in the center of each pasta circle. Fold the prepared dough in half to create a crescent shape, and press the edges together to seal. Bring a suitable pot of salted water to a boil and add the Mezzelune. Cook for about 3-5 minutes, or until they float to the surface. Drain the Mezzelune, and keep them warm. Heat the pasta sauce in a saucepan over medium heat. Toss the cooked Mezzelune in the sauce until well coated. Serve in a suitable bowl or plate and add grated Parmesan cheese on top.

Kaspressknödeln

Preparation time: 10 minutes
Cook time: 35 minutes
Nutrition facts (per serving): 300 Cal (6g fat, 34g protein, 4g fiber)

Kaspressknödeln is a traditional Austrian dish made from bread dumplings filled with a mixture of grated cheese and spices.

Ingredients (2 Servings)
1 lb. of stale bread (preferably white bread)
2 cups of whole milk
1 cup of grated Kaspress or similar cheese
½ cup of grated onions
2 cloves of garlic, minced
2 eggs
Black pepper, to taste
Salt, to taste
¼ cup of chopped parsley
3 cups of beef or chicken broth
Kaspress cheese and parsley, for garnish

Preparation
Cut the stale bread into small cubes and place in a suitable-sized mixing bowl. Heat the milk in a suitable saucepan over medium heat, and pour it over the bread cubes. Stir until the bread is well soaked. Add the grated Kaspress cheese, grated onions, minced garlic, eggs, salt, and pepper to the bread mixture. Mix well. Allow the prepared mixture to sit for about

15 minutes, until the bread has absorbed all of the liquid. Using your hands, form the prepared mixture into small dumplings. Cook the beef or chicken broth to a simmer in a suitable pot. Carefully drop the dumplings into the simmering broth and cook for about 15-20 minutes, or until they are cooked through. Remove these cooked dumplings with a slotted spoon and drain them on a paper towel. Serve the Kaspressknödeln in bowls, and ladle the broth over them. Garnish with additional grated Kaspress cheese and chopped parsley.

Canederli

Preparation time: 10 minutes

Cook time: 20 minutes

Nutrition facts (per serving): 325 Cal (10g fat, 28g protein, 3g fiber)

Canederli (also known as Knödel in German) are traditional dumplings that are typically made from stale bread, flour, and eggs.

Ingredients (4 Servings)

1 lb. of stale bread (preferably white bread)

2 cups of whole milk

3 eggs

½ cup of flour

¼ cup of parsley, chopped

1 small onion, finely chopped

Black pepper, to taste

Salt, to taste

3 cups of chicken or beef broth

Parsley, for garnish

Preparation

Cut the stale bread into small cubes and place in a suitable-sized mixing bowl. Heat the milk in a suitable saucepan over medium heat, and pour it over the bread cubes. Stir until the bread is well soaked. Add the eggs, flour, parsley, onion, salt, and pepper to the bread mixture. Mix well. Allow the prepared mixture to sit for about 15 minutes, until the bread has absorbed all of the liquid. Using your hands, form the prepared mixture into small dumplings. Bring the chicken or beef broth to a simmer in a suitable pot. Carefully drop the dumplings into the simmering broth and cook for about 15-20 minutes, or until they are cooked through. Remove these cooked dumplings with a slotted spoon and drain them on a paper towel. Serve the Canederli in bowls, and ladle the broth over them. Garnish with additional chopped parsley.

Vienna Goulash (Wiener Saftgulasch)

Preparation time: 10 minutes

Cook time: 3 hours 10 minutes

Nutrition facts (per serving): 427 Cal (23g fat, 39g protein, 5g fiber)

Wiener Saftgulasch (also known as Vienna-style juicy goulash) is a traditional Austrian dish that's made with beef, onions, and a rich gravy.

Ingredients (4 Servings)

2 lbs. of beef chuck, cut into 1-inch cubes

2 large onions, finely chopped

2 cloves of garlic, minced

2 cups of beef broth

1 cup of red wine

1 tablespoon of tomato paste

2 teaspoon of paprika

1 teaspoon of caraway seeds

Black pepper, to taste

Salt, to taste

2 tablespoons of flour

2 tablespoons of butter

2 cups of cooked egg noodles or dumplings, for serving

Preparation

In a suitable pot or Dutch oven, heat some oil over medium-high heat. Add the beef cubes and brown them on all sides. Remove the beef from the pot and set it aside. Add the onions and garlic to the pot and cook until they're softened and lightly browned. Return the beef to the pot and add the beef broth, red wine, tomato paste, paprika, and caraway seeds. Season with black pepper and salt to taste. Bring the prepared mixture to a boil, then Reduce its heat to low and cover the pot. Simmer the goulash for 2-3 hours, or until the beef is tender. In a suitable saucepan, melt the butter and stir in the flour. Slowly add some of the hot liquid from the goulash to the butter mixture, whisking constantly. Pour the prepared mixture back into the goulash and stir to combine. Cook for almost 10 minutes, or until the gravy thickens. Serve the goulash over cooked egg noodles or dumplings.

Spinach Dumplings (Pinatknödel)

Preparation time: 10 minutes

Cook time: 8 minutes

Nutrition facts (per serving): 391 Cal (13g fat, 10g protein, 1.8g fiber)

Spinatknödel (spinach dumplings) are a traditional dish from Austria and Germany. They're made by mixing spinach and breadcrumbs to form a dough, which is then shaped into dumplings and boiled.

Ingredients (2 Servings)

1 lb. of spinach, cooked and squeezed dry

½ cup of breadcrumbs

2 eggs

¼ cup of grated Parmesan cheese

¼ cup of flour

Black pepper, to taste

Salt, to taste

2 quarts of salted water, for boiling

2 tablespoons of butter, for serving

Grated Parmesan cheese, for serving

Preparation

In a suitable-sized mixing bowl, combine the cooked spinach, breadcrumbs, eggs, Parmesan cheese, flour, salt, and pepper. Mix well. Shape the prepared mixture into dumplings (about 2-3 inches in diameter). Bring a suitable pot of salted water to a boil. Gently add the dumplings to the boiling water, making sure not to overcrowd the pot. Cook the dumplings for about 6-8 minutes or until they float to the surface. Remove them with a slotted spoon, and drain them well. In a suitable pan, melt the butter over medium heat, and add the dumplings. Turn them gently to coat with butter. Serve the dumplings with grated Parmesan cheese on top.

Minced Meat Patties
(Faschierte Laibchen)

Preparation time: 10 minutes
Cook time: 5 minutes
Nutrition facts (per serving): 370 Cal (9g fat, 29g protein, 1.4g fiber)

Faschierte Laibchen (minced meat patties) are a traditional Austrian dish that's made with ground meat, breadcrumbs, and various seasonings. They're served as a main course with gravy, potatoes, and a side salad.

Ingredients (2 Servings)
1 lb. of ground beef or pork
½ cup of breadcrumbs
1 onion, finely chopped
2 cloves of garlic, minced
2 eggs
2 tablespoons of parsley, chopped
2 tablespoons of chives, chopped
1 teaspoon of caraway seeds
Black pepper, to taste
Salt, to taste
Flour, for dusting
Oil, for frying

Preparation
In a suitable-sized mixing bowl, combine the ground meat, breadcrumbs, onion, garlic, eggs, parsley, chives, caraway seeds, salt, and pepper. Mix

well. Shape the prepared mixture into small patties (about 3-4 inches in diameter). Dust the patties with flour. In a suitable pan, heat some oil over medium-high heat. Add the patties to the pan and fry them for about 4-5 minutes per side or until golden brown and cooked through. Drain the patties on a paper towel. Serve the Faschierte Laibchen with gravy, potatoes, and a side salad.

Beuschel

Preparation time: 10 minutes

Cook time: 1 hour 15 minutes

Nutrition facts (per serving): 320 Cal (6g fat, 31g protein, 1g fiber)

Beuschel is a traditional Austrian dish made from veal lung, heart, and spleen, which are cooked in a creamy sauce. It's considered as a typical dish of Viennese cuisine.

Ingredients (2 Servings)

1 lb. of veal lung, heart, and spleen, cleaned and diced

1 onion, finely chopped

2 cloves of garlic, minced

2 cups of beef or veal broth

1 cup of heavy cream

2 tablespoons of flour

Black pepper, to taste

Salt, to taste

2 tablespoons of butter

1 tablespoon of parsley, chopped

Preparation

In a suitable pot, sauté the onions and garlic in butter over medium heat until softened. Add the diced veal lung, heart, and spleen to the pot and sauté for a few minutes until browned. Add the dry flour and stir well to coat the meat. Slowly pour in the beef or veal broth and bring the prepared mixture to a boil. Reduce its heat and let the prepared mixture simmer for about 1 hour or until the meat is tender. Stir in the cream and season with black pepper and salt to taste. Simmer for 10-15 minutes or until the sauce is thickened. Stir in the chopped parsley and serve the Beuschel hot, with mashed potatoes or bread dumplings.

Zwiebelrostbraten

Preparation time: 10 minutes

Cook time: 30 minutes

Nutrition facts (per serving): 421 Cal (10g fat, 26g protein, 1.7g fiber)

Zwiebelrostbraten is a traditional Austrian dish that consists of a suitable pan-fried beef steak topped with caramelized onions and served with gravy. It's a classic dish that can be found in many traditional Austrian restaurants.

Ingredients (2 Servings)

2 beef steaks (sirloin or rump steak)

Black pepper, to taste

Salt, to taste

Flour, for dusting

4 tablespoons of butter

2 large onions, thinly sliced

2 cups of beef or veal broth

2 tablespoons of flour

1 tablespoon of parsley, chopped

Preparation

Season the steaks with black pepper and salt and dust them with flour. In a suitable pan, melt 2 tablespoons of butter over high heat. Add the beef steaks to the pan and cook them for about 2-3 minutes per side or until browned and cooked to your desired level of doneness. Remove these steaks from the pan and set them aside to rest. In the same pan, melt the remaining 2 tablespoons of butter over medium heat. Toss in the sliced onions to the pan and sauté them until they're caramelized and golden brown. Remove the onions from the pan and set them aside. In the same pan, add 2 cups of beef or veal broth and 2 tablespoons of flour. Whisk well to combine. Bring the prepared mixture to a boil and let it simmer until it thickens. Season the gravy with black pepper and salt to taste. Slice the steaks and place them on a serving platter. Top the steaks with the caramelized onions and pour the gravy over the top. Garnish with chopped parsley and serve with mashed potatoes or spatzle.

Backhendl

Preparation time: 10 minutes

Cook time: 12 minutes

Nutrition facts (per serving): 228 Cal (8g fat, 28g protein, 1.8g fiber)

Backhendl is a traditional Austrian dish that consists of deep-fried chicken. It's a popular dish in Austria and is often found on the menu of traditional Austrian restaurants.

Ingredients (4 Servings)

4 chicken legs

Black pepper, to taste

Salt, to taste

1 cup of flour

2 eggs, beaten

1 cup of breadcrumbs

Oil, for frying

Preparation

Season the chicken legs with black pepper and salt. Place the flour, beaten eggs, and breadcrumbs in separate bowls. Dip each chicken leg in the flour, then the eggs, and finally the breadcrumbs, making sure to coat each leg evenly. Heat oil in a suitable pan over medium-high heat. Add the chicken legs to the pan and fry them for about 10-12 minutes or until golden brown and cooked through. Drain the chicken legs on a paper towel to remove any excess oil. Serve the Backhendl with a side of potato salad or roasted potatoes and a sprinkle of parsley.

Tafelspitz

Preparation time: 10 minutes

Cook time: 2 hours 30 minutes

Nutrition facts (per serving): 411 Cal (5g fat, 19g protein, 2g fiber)

Tafelspitz is a traditional Austrian dish made from boiled beef, typically taken from the top round cut of the beef, and served with a variety of accompaniments such as boiled potatoes, root vegetables, and horseradish sauce.

Ingredients (6 Servings)

3 lbs. of beef (preferably from the top round)

2 medium-sized onions, chopped

2 carrots, chopped

2 celery stalks, chopped

1 bay leaf

3 cloves of garlic

1 teaspoon whole black peppercorns

Salt

Preparation

Rinse the beef and pat it dry. In a suitable pot, add the beef, chopped onions, carrots, celery stalks, bay leaf, garlic, peppercorns, salt and enough water to cover the beef. Bring the prepared mixture to a boil, then Reduce its heat and let it simmer for about 2 to 2.5 hours, or until the beef is tender. Remove the cooked beef from the pot and let it cool for about 10 minutes. Slice the beef against the grain, into thin slices. Serve the Tafelspitz hot with boiled potatoes and a traditional Austrian sauce, such as a remoulade or a horseradish sauce. Enjoy!

Creamy Austrian Rice with Peas and Onion

Preparation time: 10 minutes
Cook time: 23 minutes
Nutrition facts (per serving): 310 Cal (4g fat, 9g protein, 1.1g fiber)

Creamy Austrian rice with peas and onion is a traditional dish made by cooking rice with peas and onions in a creamy sauce. The dish typically starts with sautéed onions and then adding cooked rice, peas, and a mixture of milk and cream to the pan. The mixture is then simmered until the sauce has thickened and the rice is fully cooked.

Ingredients (4 Servings)

1 cup of long grain rice
1 cup of frozen peas
1 large onion, diced
2 cups of vegetable or chicken broth
2 cups of heavy cream
Salt, to taste
Black pepper, to taste
Butter or oil, for cooking

Preparation

In a suitable saucepan, heat the butter or oil over medium heat. Add the diced onion and cook until it is soft. Add the rice to the saucepan and stir to combine it with the onion. Cook until the rice is slightly toasted. Pour in the broth and stir to combine. Bring the prepared mixture to a boil, then Reduce its heat and let it simmer for about 18 to 20 minutes, or until the rice is tender. Stir in the frozen peas and cook for another 2-3 minutes, or until the peas are heated through. Stir in the cream and season with black pepper and salt to taste. Serve the creamy Austrian rice with peas and onion hot. Enjoy!

Austrian Rice with Beef (Reisfleisch)

Preparation time: 10 minutes
Cook time: 20 minutes
Nutrition facts (per serving): 423 Cal (4g fat, 25g protein, 1.2g fiber)

Austrian Reisfleisch is a traditional Austrian dish made from cooked rice and beef, simmered together in a flavorful broth. The beef is typically diced or sliced and browned in a pan, then simmered with the rice, onions, and broth to make a hearty and flavorful stew.

Ingredients (2 Servings)
1 cup of long grain rice
1 lb. of beef or pork, diced
1 large onion, diced
2 carrots, diced
2 celery stalks, diced
2 cups of beef or chicken broth
Salt, to taste
Black pepper, to taste
Butter or oil, for cooking

Preparation
In a suitable saucepan, heat the butter or oil over medium heat. Add the diced onion and cook until it's soft. Add the diced meat to the saucepan and cook until browned on all sides. Add the diced carrots and celery to the saucepan and cook for 2-3 minutes, or until the vegetables are slightly

softened. Stir in the rice and cook for 1-2 minutes, or until the rice is slightly toasted. Pour in the broth and stir to combine. Bring the prepared mixture to a boil, then Reduce its heat and let it simmer for about 18 to 20 minutes, or until the rice is tender. Season with black pepper and salt to taste. Serve the Reisfleisch hot. Enjoy!

Garlic Butter Rice

Preparation time: 10 minutes
Cook time: 30 minutes
Nutrition facts (per serving): 227 Cal (8g fat, 5g protein, 2g fiber)

Garlic butter rice is a dish made by cooking rice in a mixture of butter and garlic, giving it a rich, fragrant flavor. The rice is typically cooked in a saucepan with butter and minced garlic, and may also include additional ingredients such as chicken or vegetable broth, white wine, or grated cheese to add flavor and texture.

Ingredients (2 Servings)
1 cup of long grain rice
2 cups of water
Salt, to taste
2 tablespoons of unsalted butter
2 cloves of garlic, minced
2 tablespoons of chopped fresh parsley, optional

Preparation
Rinse the long grain rice in a fine-mesh strainer until the water runs clear. In a suitable saucepan, bring the water to a boil and add a pinch of salt. Stir in the rice and Reduce its heat to low. Cover the saucepan and let it simmer for about 18-20 minutes, or until the rice is tender and the water has been absorbed. Remove the saucepan from heat and let it sit, covered, for 5 minutes. In a suitable saucepan, melt the butter over medium heat. Toss in the minced garlic and cook until fragrant, about 1-2 minutes. Stir

the garlic butter into the cooked rice and mix well. Serve the garlic butter rice hot, garnished with chopped parsley if desired. Enjoy!

Stuffed Peppers with Ground Meat

Preparation time: 10 minutes
Cook time: 50 minutes
Nutrition facts (per serving): 397 Cal (21g fat, 23g protein, 5g fiber)

Stuffed peppers with ground meat is a dish made by filling bell peppers with a mixture of ground meat, rice, and other ingredients, then baking them until tender and flavorful. The filling is typically made by browning ground beef or a mixture of beef and pork in a pan with onions, then adding cooked rice and a variety of seasonings such as salt, pepper, paprika, or herbs.

Ingredients (6 Servings)
6 large bell peppers
1 lb. of ground beef or turkey
1 large onion, diced
2 cloves of garlic, minced
1 cup of cooked rice
1 can of diced tomatoes (14.5 oz)
1 teaspoon of dried basil
1 teaspoon of dried oregano
Salt, to taste
Black pepper, to taste
1 cup of shredded cheese
Olive oil, for cooking

Preparation

At 376 degrees F, preheat your oven. Chop the tops of the bell peppers off and remove the seeds and membranes. In a suitable skillet, heat the olive oil over medium heat. Add the diced onion and cook until it's soft. Toss in the minced garlic and cook for another 30 seconds, or until fragrant. Add the ground beef and saute until browned, breaking it up into small pieces as it cooks. Stir in the cooked rice, diced tomatoes, basil, oregano, salt, and pepper. Cook for 2-3 minutes, or until the prepared mixture is heated through. Spoon the meat mixture into the hollowed out bell peppers and place them in a large baking dish. Bake your stuffed peppers in the oven for 25-30 minutes, or until they're tender and the filling is hot. Sprinkle shredded cheese over the stuffed peppers and return to the oven for another 5-10 minutes, or until the cheese is melted and bubbly. Serve the stuffed peppers hot. Enjoy!

Djuvech

Preparation time: 10 minutes
Cook time: 30 minutes
Nutrition facts (per serving): 327 Cal (20g fat, 21g protein, 3g fiber)

Here's a type of pilaf made with rice, vegetables, and meat, typically chicken or beef. The dish is made by first sautéing diced onions and vegetables, such as carrots and bell peppers, in a pan. Then, the rice is added and simmered in a flavorful broth made from meat and spices such as paprika, bay leaves, and thyme. The mixture is then covered and baked in the oven until the rice is tender and fully cooked.

Ingredients (4 Servings)
1 cup of long grain rice
1 large onion, diced
2 cloves of garlic, minced
2 medium carrots, diced
2 medium potatoes, diced
1 medium zucchini, diced
1 can of diced tomatoes (14.5 oz)
2 cups of vegetable broth
Salt, to taste
Black pepper, to taste
1 paprika
Olive oil, for cooking

Preparation

In a suitable saucepan, heat the olive oil over medium heat. Add the diced onion and cook until it is soft. Toss in the minced garlic and cook for another 30 seconds, or until fragrant. Stir in the diced carrots and potatoes and cook for 2-3 minutes, or until the vegetables are slightly softened. Stir in the diced zucchini and cook for another 2-3 minutes, or until the zucchini is slightly softened. Add in the can of diced tomatoes and paprika, and cook for 2-3 minutes, or until the prepared mixture is heated through. Stir in the rice and pour in the vegetable broth. Bring the prepared mixture to a boil, then reduce its heat and let it simmer for about 18-20 minutes, or until the rice is tender and the liquid has been absorbed. Season with black pepper and salt to taste. Serve the Djuvec hot. Enjoy!

Prawn Machbous

Preparation time: 10 minutes
Cook time: 25 minutes
Nutrition facts (per serving): 308 Cal (8g fat, 31g protein, 2g fiber)

Prawn Machbous is a dish made from cooked prawns, served with a flavorful mixture of spices and herbs on a bed of steamed rice. The prawns are typically cooked with a mixture of spices such as cumin, paprika, coriander, and turmeric, along with ingredients such as garlic, ginger, and onions. The cooked prawns are then served on a bed of steamed rice, which is often flavored with spices such as saffron, cinnamon, and cardamom.

Ingredients (4 Servings)
1 lb. of large prawns, peeled and deveined
1 cup of long grain rice
1 large onion, diced
2 cloves of garlic, minced
1 teaspoon of cumin
1 teaspoon of paprika
Salt, to taste
Black pepper, to taste
1 cup of canned diced tomatoes
1 cup of chicken or vegetable broth
2 tablespoons of olive oil
Lemon wedges, for serving

Preparation

In a suitable saucepan, heat the olive oil over medium heat. Add the diced onion and cook until it's soft. Toss in the minced garlic and cook for another 30 seconds, or until fragrant. Stir in the cumin and paprika, and cook for another 30 seconds, or until fragrant. Stir in the canned diced tomatoes and cook for 2-3 minutes, or until the prepared mixture is heated through. Stir in the rice, prawns, salt, pepper, and broth. Bring the prepared mixture to a boil, then Reduce its heat and let it simmer, covered, for about 20 minutes until the liquid has been absorbed. Serve the Prawn Machbous hot with lemon wedges on the side. Enjoy!

Austrian Veal Roulades

Preparation time: 10 minutes
Cook time: 25 minutes
Nutrition facts (per serving): 419 Cal (11g fat, 23g protein, 1.3g fiber)

Austrian Veal Roulades is a dish made with thin slices of veal stuffed with cheese, ham, and spices.

Ingredients (4 Servings)
8 thin slices of veal (about 1.5 lbs.)
8 thin slices of ham
8 thin slices of cheese (such as Gouda or Emmental)
Salt, to taste
Black pepper, to taste
Paprika, to taste
2 tablespoons of butter
1 large onion, diced
2 cloves of garlic, minced
2 cups of beef broth
2 tablespoons of flour
½ cup of sour cream
2 tablespoons of chopped fresh parsley

Preparation
Place a slice of ham, cheese, salt, pepper, and paprika on top of each slice of veal. Roll the veal up tightly and secure each roulade with toothpicks. In a suitable skillet, heat the butter over medium heat. Add the diced

onion and cook until it is soft. Toss in the minced garlic and cook for another 30 seconds, or until fragrant. Place the veal roulades in the skillet and brown on all sides. Pour in the beef broth and bring the prepared mixture to a boil. Reduce its heat and let it simmer, covered, for about 20-25 minutes, or until the veal is cooked through. In a suitable-sized bowl, whisk together the flour and sour cream until smooth. Stir the flour-sour cream mixture into the skillet and cook until the sauce thickens. Serve the Austrian Veal Roulades hot, topped with the sauce and chopped parsley. Enjoy!

Kraufleckerl Austrian Noodles with Cabbage

Preparation time: 10 minutes
Cook time: 25 minutes
Nutrition facts (per serving): 338 Cal (3g fat, 8g protein, 3.4g fiber)

Krautfleckerl is a traditional Austrian dish made from sauerkraut and pasta, similar to Italian pasta and sauerkraut dishes. The sauerkraut is simmered with bacon and onions until tender and flavorful, and then mixed with cooked egg noodles to make the dish.

Ingredients (6 Servings)
1 lb. of egg noodles
1 large head of cabbage, chopped
2 tablespoons of butter
1 large onion, diced
2 cloves of garlic, minced
Salt, to taste
Black pepper, to taste
1 teaspoon of caraway seeds
2 cups of chicken or vegetable broth
2 tablespoons of flour
½ cup of sour cream

Preparation
Cook the egg noodles as per the package instructions and set aside. In a suitable skillet, heat the butter over medium heat. Add the diced onion

and cook until it is soft. Toss in the minced garlic and cook for another 30 seconds, or until fragrant. Stir in the chopped cabbage, salt, pepper, and caraway seeds. Cook until the cabbage is tender. Stir in the chicken broth and bring the prepared mixture to a boil. Reduce its heat and let it simmer, covered, for about 15-20 minutes, or until the cabbage is soft. In a suitable-sized bowl, whisk together the flour and sour cream until smooth. Stir the flour-sour cream mixture into the skillet and cook until the sauce thickens. Serve the Krautfleckerl by placing a serving of egg noodles on a plate and topping with the cabbage mixture. Enjoy!

Steirisches Wurzelfleisch

Preparation time: 10 minutes

Cook time: 1 hour 30 minutes

Nutrition facts (per serving): 334 Cal (10g fat, 32g protein, 4.4g fiber)

Steirisches Wurzelfleisch is a traditional Austrian dish made with beef and root vegetables.

Ingredients (4 Servings)

1 ½ lbs. of beef, cut into cubes

1 large onion, diced

2 large carrots, peeled and diced

2 large parsnips, peeled and diced

2 large potatoes, peeled and diced

1 teaspoon of caraway seeds

Salt, to taste

Black pepper, to taste

2 tablespoons of flour

2 cups of beef broth

2 tablespoons of butter

Preparation

In a suitable pot, heat the butter over medium heat. Add the diced onion and cook until it's soft. Stir in the cubed beef and cook until browned on all sides. Stir in the diced carrots, parsnips, and potatoes. Season with caraway seeds, salt, and pepper. Sprinkle the flour over the prepared mixture and stir to combine. Pour in the beef broth and bring the prepared mixture to a boil. Reduce its heat and let it simmer, covered, for about 1 ½ hours, or until the beef is tender and the vegetables are cooked through. Serve the Steirisches Wurzelfleisch hot, with crusty bread or boiled potatoes. Enjoy!

Austrian Roasted Goose

Preparation time: 10 minutes
Cook time: 2 hours 30 minutes
Nutrition facts (per serving): 375 Cal (12g fat, 34g protein, 6g fiber)

Austrian roasted goose is a traditional dish made from a whole roasted goose, typically served as a holiday meal or special occasion. The goose is seasoned with salt, pepper, and other spices, and then roasted in the oven until crispy and golden. It's often served with traditional Austrian accompaniments, such as roasted potatoes and red cabbage, as well as gravy made from the pan drippings.

Ingredients (8 Servings)
1 whole goose (about 4 lbs.)
Salt, to taste
Black pepper, to taste
2 onions, chopped
4 cloves of garlic, minced
2 apples, peeled and sliced
1 teaspoon of dried thyme
1 teaspoon of dried rosemary
½ teaspoon of nutmeg
½ teaspoon of allspice
1 cup white wine

Preparation

At 376 degrees F, preheat your oven. Clean the goose inside and out and pat dry. Season generously with black pepper and salt. In a suitable roasting pan, place the chopped onions and sliced apples on the bottom of the pan. Place the goose on top, breast-side up. Mix together the minced garlic, dried thyme, dried rosemary, nutmeg, and allspice. Rub this mixture all over the goose. Pour the white wine into the bottom of the roasting pan. Cover the roasting pan with foil and place in the oven. Bake for 1 hour and 30 minutes. After 1 hour and 30 minutes, remove the foil from the roasting pan. Baste the goose with the juices from the bottom of the pan. Return the roasting pan to the oven and bake for another hour, or until the internal temperature of the goose reaches 165°F (74°C). Once done, remove it from the oven and let rest for 10 minutes before carving and serving. Enjoy!

Beet Golusch

Preparation time: 10 minutes
Cook time: 20 minutes
Nutrition facts (per serving): 451 Cal (7g fat, 35g protein, 2.4g fiber)

Beet goulash is a type of goulash made with beets as the main ingredient. In the case of beet goulash, the beets are peeled, diced, and simmered with other vegetables such as onions and carrots, and sometimes with meat or other ingredients such as potatoes or sour cream.

Ingredients (4 Servings)

2 lbs. of beets, peeled and grated
2 tablespoons of butter
1 onion, finely chopped
2 cloves of garlic, minced
2 tablespoons of flour
2 cups of beef or vegetable broth
1 cup of heavy cream
Salt, to taste
Black pepper, to taste
2 tablespoons of red wine vinegar, optional
2 tablespoons of chopped fresh dill or parsley, optional

Preparation

In a suitable saucepan, melt the butter over medium heat. Add the chopped onion and minced garlic and cook until soft, about 5 minutes. Add the grated beets to the saucepan and cook for 5 minutes, stirring occasionally. Sprinkle the flour over the beets and stir to combine. Cook for 2 minutes. Gradually add the broth, stirring constantly, until the prepared mixture comes to a boil. Reduce heat to low and cook on a simmer for 10 minutes, stirring occasionally. Stir in the heavy cream and continue to simmer for 5 minutes. Season them well with black pepper and salt to taste. If desired, stir in the red wine vinegar and chopped dill or parsley. Serve hot as a soup or over potatoes, rice, or crusty bread. Enjoy!

Chicken Schnitzel

Preparation time: 10 minutes
Cook time: 6 minutes
Nutrition facts (per serving): 378 Cal (14g fat, 39g protein, 2.4g fiber)

Chicken schnitzel is a popular dish in German-speaking countries and other parts of Europe. It's made by coating thin slices of boneless chicken in breadcrumbs and frying them until they're golden brown and crispy.

Ingredients (4 servings)
4 boneless, skinless chicken breasts
Salt, to taste
Black pepper, to taste
2 cups of all-purpose flour
4 large eggs, beaten
2 cups of breadcrumbs
½ teaspoon of paprika
Vegetable oil, for frying
Lemon wedges, for serving

Preparation
Pound the boneless chicken breasts with a meat mallet to an even thickness. Season with black pepper and salt. Spread the flour in a shallow dish, add the beaten eggs to another shallow dish, and spread the breadcrumbs mixed with paprika in a third shallow dish. Coat each chicken breast in the flour, shaking off any excess. Dip in the beaten eggs, then coat in the breadcrumbs. In a suitable deep skillet, heat about ½ inch

of vegetable oil over medium-high heat until hot but not smoking. Add the chicken schnitzel to the skillet and cook for 2-3 minutes per side, or until golden brown and crispy. Drain on paper towels and season with additional salt. Serve hot with lemon wedges. Enjoy!

Veal Schnitzel

Preparation time: 10 minutes
Cook time: 12 minutes
Nutrition facts (per serving): 398 Cal (9g fat, 23g protein, 2.1g fiber)

Veal schnitzel is a dish made from thin, pounded slices of veal that are breaded and fried until crispy and golden brown. Like chicken schnitzel, veal schnitzel is a popular dish in German-speaking countries and in other parts of Europe.

Ingredients (4 servings)
4 veal cutlets, pounded to an even thickness
Salt, to taste
Black pepper, to taste
2 cups of all-purpose flour
4 large eggs, beaten
2 cups of breadcrumbs
½ teaspoon of paprika
Vegetable oil, for frying
Lemon wedges, for serving

Preparation
Season the veal cutlets with black pepper and salt. Set up your breading station by spread the flour in a shallow dish, adding the beaten eggs to another shallow dish, and the breadcrumbs mixed with paprika in a third shallow dish. Coat each cutlet in the flour, shaking off any excess. Dip in the beaten eggs, then coat in the breadcrumbs. In suitable deep skillet,

heat about ½ inch of vegetable oil over medium-high heat until hot but not smoking. Add the veal schnitzel to the skillet and cook for 2-3 minutes per side, or until golden brown and crispy. Drain on paper towels and season with additional salt. Serve hot with lemon wedges. Enjoy!

Stuffed Cabbage Leaves with Paprika Tomato Sauce

Preparation time: 10 minutes
Cook time: 60 minutes
Nutrition facts (per serving): 411 Cal (12g fat, 20g protein, 3g fiber)

Stuffed cabbage leaves with paprika tomato sauce is a traditional dish in Eastern European cuisine. It's made by stuffing tender cabbage leaves with a filling of ground meat, rice, and spices, and then simmering them in a flavorful tomato sauce. The sauce is typically seasoned with paprika, which gives it a distinctive smoky flavor, as well as with other ingredients such as garlic, onions, and herbs.

Ingredients (4-6 servings)
1 large head of green cabbage
1 lb. of ground beef or pork
1 cup of cooked rice
1 onion, finely chopped
2 cloves of garlic, minced
Salt, to taste
Black pepper, to taste
1 tablespoon of paprika
1 can of diced tomatoes (14.5 oz)
1 cup of beef or vegetable broth
1 tablespoon of tomato paste
1 tablespoon of red wine vinegar
2 tablespoons of olive oil
Fresh parsley, chopped, for garnish

Preparation

At 350 degrees F, preheat your oven. Cut out the core and blanch the remaining leaves in boiling water for 2-3 minutes, or until soft and pliable. In a suitable-sized bowl, mix together the ground beef or pork, cooked rice, chopped onion, minced garlic, salt, pepper, and 1 teaspoon of paprika. Lay out a blanched cabbage leaf and place 2-3 tablespoons of the meat mixture in the center. Roll up the cabbage leaf, tucking in the sides, to form a neat cylinder. Repeat with the remaining leaves and meat mixture. In a suitable saucepan, heat the olive oil over medium heat. Add the remaining paprika and cook for 30 seconds, or until fragrant. Stir in the diced tomatoes, broth, tomato paste, and red wine vinegar. Cook to a boil, then reduce heat to low and cook on a simmer for 10-15 minutes, or until slightly thickened. Arrange the cabbage rolls in a single layer in a large baking dish. Pour the tomato sauce over the top. Cover this dish with aluminum foil and bake for 45 minutes, or until the cabbage is tender and the filling is cooked through. Serve hot, garnished with chopped parsley if desired. Enjoy!

Veal Chop Holstein Schnitzel

Preparation time: 10 minutes
Cook time: 12 minutes
Nutrition facts (per serving): 426 Cal (14g fat, 21g protein, 4g fiber)

Veal Chop Holstein Schnitzel is a classic German dish that consists of a breaded and fried veal cutlet served with a sunny-side-up egg and anchovy fillets on top. The dish is typically garnished with capers and lemon wedges, and is often served with a side of French fries or boiled potatoes. The name "Holstein" refers to the black and white coloring of the dish, which is meant to resemble the coat of a Holstein cow.

Ingredients (4 servings)

4 veal chops
Salt, to taste
Black pepper, to taste
2 cups of all-purpose flour
4 large eggs, beaten
2 cups of breadcrumbs
½ teaspoon of paprika
Vegetable oil, for frying
4 slices of ham
4 slices of Emmental or Swiss cheese
4 lemon wedges, for serving
4 tablespoons of capers, for serving

Preparation

Season the veal chops with black pepper and salt. Set up a breading station by placing the flour in a shallow dish, the beaten eggs in another shallow dish, and the breadcrumbs mixed with paprika in a third shallow dish. Coat each chop in the flour, shaking off any excess. Dip in the beaten eggs, then coat in the breadcrumbs. In a suitable deep skillet, heat about ½ inch of vegetable oil over medium-high heat until hot but not smoking. Add the crusted veal chops to the skillet and cook for 2-3 minutes per side, or until golden brown and crispy. Drain on paper towels. Top each veal chop with a slice of ham and a slice of cheese. Return to the skillet and cook for 1-2 minutes, or until the cheese is melted. Serve hot with lemon wedges and capers on the side. Enjoy!

Rib Eye with Mustard, Crispy Onion and Herbs

Preparation time: 10 minutes

Cook time: 23 minutes

Nutrition facts (per serving): 427 Cal (10g fat, 29g protein, 1.2g fiber)

Rib eye with mustard, crispy onion, and herbs is a dish that typically consists of a grilled or pan-fried rib eye steak served with a sauce made from mustard, herbs, and crispy fried onions. The rib eye steak is a flavorful and tender cut of beef that is known for its rich marbling, and is often seasoned with salt and pepper before cooking

Ingredients (4 servings)

4 boneless rib eye steaks (1-inch thick)

Salt, to taste

Black pepper, to taste

2 tablespoons of olive oil

2 onions, thinly sliced

¼ cup of all-purpose flour

2 tablespoons of grainy mustard

2 tablespoons of chopped fresh parsley

2 tablespoons of chopped fresh thyme

2 tablespoons of chopped fresh rosemary

2 tablespoons of butter

Preparation

Season the rib eye steaks with black pepper and salt. In a suitable skillet, heat the olive oil over medium heat. Add the sliced onions and cook for 10-15 minutes, or until golden brown and crispy, stirring occasionally. Remove from the skillet and set aside. In a suitable dish, mix together the flour, mustard, parsley, thyme, and rosemary. Dip each steak in the flour mixture, pressing to coat both sides. In that same skillet, melt the butter over medium-high heat. Add the steaks and cook for 3-4 minutes per side, or until desired doneness. Serve the steaks topped with the crispy onions and any remaining herb mixture. Enjoy!

Mussels Mariniere

Preparation time: 10 minutes
Cook time: 15 minutes
Nutrition facts (per serving): 421 Cal (8g fat, 18g protein, 2g fiber)

Mussels mariniere is a classic French dish that consists of mussels cooked in a flavorful broth made from white wine, shallots, garlic, and herbs. The mussels are steamed in the broth until they open, and the broth is then used to flavor the dish.

Ingredients (4 servings)
2 lbs. of fresh mussels, scrubbed and debearded
4 cloves of garlic, minced
1 shallot, minced
½ cup of white wine
¼ cup of chicken or fish stock
2 tablespoons of butter
2 tablespoons of chopped fresh parsley
Salt, to taste
Black pepper, to taste

Preparation
In a suitable pot, sauté the garlic and shallot in the butter over medium heat until fragrant, about 2 minutes. Add the white wine and chicken or fish stock. Cook to a boil and then reduce heat to low. Add the mussels to the pot, cover with a lid, and cook for 5-7 minutes, or until the mussels have opened. Discard any mussels that do not open. Season with black pepper and salt to taste. Stir in the chopped parsley. Serve the mussels in bowls with the cooking liquid. Enjoy with crusty bread to soak up the sauce.

Beef Rouladen with Brunoise Vegetables and Red Wine

Preparation time: 10 minutes
Cook time: 1 hour 5 minutes
Nutrition facts (per serving): 308 Cal (8g fat, 33g protein, 4g fiber)

Beef Rouladen with brunoise vegetables and red wine is a classic German dish that consists of thin slices of beef that are rolled around a filling of diced vegetables, pickles, and bacon, and then simmered in a red wine sauce. The vegetables in the filling are usually diced into small, uniform pieces, a technique called "brunoise," and the beef is usually pounded thin before being rolled.

Ingredients (4 servings
4 thin slices of beef sirloin
4 slices of bacon
1 onion, diced
1 carrot, diced
1 stalk of celery, diced
1 tablespoon of all-purpose flour
1 cup of red wine
1 cup of beef broth
Salt, to taste
Black pepper, to taste
4 tablespoons of Dijon mustard
4 pickles, sliced

Preparation

Place a slice of bacon, a spoonful of onion, carrot, and celery (brunoise), a dollop of mustard, and a few pickle slices on top of each slice of beef. Roll up the beef, securing with a toothpick or kitchen twine. In a suitable skillet, brown the beef rouladen on all sides in a little bit of oil over medium-high heat. Remove from the skillet and set aside. Add the diced onion, carrot, and celery to the skillet and sauté until softened, about 5 minutes. Stir in the flour and cook for another minute. Pour in the red wine and beef broth, stirring to combine. Return the beef rouladen to the skillet and cook to a boil. Reduce heat to low, cover the skillet with a lid, and cook on a simmer for 1 hour, or until the beef is tender and cooked through. Season with black pepper and salt to taste. Serve the rouladen hot with the sauce on the side. Enjoy!

Pork Chops with Cabbage and Sherry Vinegar Sauce

Preparation time: 10 minutes
Cook time: 30 minutes
Nutrition facts (per serving): 431 Cal (7g fat, 29g protein, 2.4g fiber)

Pork chops with cabbage and sherry vinegar sauce is a dish that typically consists of pan-fried or grilled pork chops served with a side of sautéed cabbage and a sauce made from sherry vinegar, onions, and herbs. The pork chops are seasoned with salt and pepper and then cooked until they are browned on the outside and juicy and tender on the inside.

Ingredients (4 servings)
4 bone-in pork chops
Salt, to taste
Black pepper, to taste
2 tablespoons of olive oil
1 head of green cabbage, thinly sliced
1 onion, diced
2 cloves of garlic, minced
¼ cup sherry vinegar
½ cup of chicken broth
2 tablespoons of unsalted butter
1 tablespoon sugar
2 tablespoons of chopped fresh parsley

Preparation

Season the pork chops with black pepper and salt. In a suitable skillet, heat the olive oil over medium-high heat. Add the pork chops and cook for 4-5 minutes per side, or until browned and crispy. Remove from the skillet and set aside. In the same skillet, add the sliced cabbage, onion, and garlic. Cook until softened, about 5 minutes. Stir in the sherry vinegar, chicken broth, butter, and sugar. Return the pork chops to the skillet, nestling them into the cabbage mixture. Cover the skillet with a lid and cook on a simmer for 10-15 minutes, or until the pork is cooked through and the sauce has thickened slightly. Season with black pepper and salt to taste. Stir in the chopped parsley. Serve the pork chops hot with the cabbage mixture and sauce on the side.

Bacon Onion Spaetzle

Preparation time: 10 minutes

Cook time: 20 minutes

Nutrition facts (per serving): 301 Cal (8g fat, 2g protein, 1.1g fiber)

Bacon Onion Spaetzle is a German dish that combines the soft and tender egg noodle-like pasta called spaetzle with crispy bacon and caramelized onions. The spaetzle is made from a simple batter of eggs, flour, and milk, which is then dropped into boiling water and cooked until it floats to the surface.

Ingredients (4 servings)

1 cup of all-purpose flour

½ teaspoon of salt

3 large eggs

½ cup of milk

2 tablespoons of butter

1 large onion, thinly sliced

8 ounces of bacon, diced

Black pepper, to taste

2 tablespoons of chopped fresh parsley

Preparation

In a suitable-sized bowl, whisk together the flour, salt, eggs, and milk to form a batter. In a suitable pot of boiling salted water, use a spaetzle maker or a colander with large holes to drop spoonfuls of the batter into the water. Cook these spaetzle for 2-3 minutes until they float to the surface. Remove the cooked spaetzle with a slotted spoon and set aside. In a suitable skillet, melt the butter over medium heat. Toss in the onion and bacon and cook until softened and crispy, about 10 minutes. Add the cooked spaetzle to the skillet and toss to combine with the bacon and onion. Season with black pepper and salt to taste. Serve the spaetzle hot with the bacon and onion mixture on top. Sprinkle with the chopped parsley. Enjoy!

Jaeger Schnitzel

Preparation time: 10 minutes

Cook time: 14 minutes

Nutrition facts (per serving): 413 Cal (7g fat, 34g protein, 4.4g fiber)

Jäger Schnitzel is a traditional German dish that consists of a breaded and fried veal or pork cutlet that is topped with a creamy mushroom sauce. The cutlet is first pounded thin, then coated in flour, beaten egg, and breadcrumbs, and fried until crispy and golden brown.

Ingredients (4 Servings)

4 boneless pork cutlets (1-inch thick)

Black pepper, to taste

Salt, to taste

1 cup all-purpose flour

2 large eggs

1 cup breadcrumbs

½ cup vegetable oil

½ cup chopped onions

½ cup beef broth

½ cup heavy cream

1 teaspoon lemon juice

2 tablespoons chopped fresh parsley

Preparation

Season the pork cutlets with black pepper and salt. Put the flour, eggs, and breadcrumbs in separate shallow dishes. Coat each cutlet in flour, then dip in eggs, and coat with breadcrumbs. Heat the oil in a suitable skillet over medium heat. Add the pork cutlets to the skillet and cook until golden brown, about 3-4 minutes per side. Remove the cutlets from the skillet and set aside. Toss in the onions to the skillet and cook until soft, about 2-3 minutes. Add the beef broth and lemon juice to the skillet and cook to a boil. Reduce heat to low and stir in the heavy cream. Return the pork cutlets to the skillet and cook until heated through, about 2-3 minutes. Serve the schnitzel with the sauce and sprinkled with fresh parsley. Enjoy!

Pork Schnitzel

Preparation time: 10 minutes
Cook time: 12 minutes
Nutrition facts (per serving): 368 Cal (9g fat, 31g protein, 1.4g fiber)

Pork Schnitzel is a dish that is popular in Germany and Austria. It is made by pounding thin slices of pork tenderloin or boneless pork chops to an even thickness, then coating the slices in flour, beaten eggs, and breadcrumbs. The coated pork slices are then pan-fried until they're golden brown and crispy.

Ingredients (4 Servings)

4 boneless pork cutlets (¼ inch thick)
Black pepper, to taste
Salt, to taste
1 cup all-purpose flour
2 large eggs, beaten
1 ½ cups breadcrumbs
¼ cup vegetable oil
Lemon wedges, for serving

Preparation

Season the pork cutlets with black pepper and salt. Put the flour in one shallow dish, the beaten eggs in another, and the breadcrumbs in a third. Coat each pork cutlet in the flour, then dip in the beaten eggs, and coat in the breadcrumbs. Heat the oil in a suitable skillet over medium-high heat. Add the pork cutlets to the skillet and cook until golden brown, about 3-4 minutes per side. Remove the cutlets from the skillet and drain on paper towels. Serve the schnitzel hot with lemon wedges on the side. Enjoy!

Paprika Chicken Schnitzel with Fried Eggs (Holstein)

Preparation time: 10 minutes
Cook time: 12 minutes
Nutrition facts (per serving): 407 Cal (5g fat, 27g protein, 1.5g fiber)

Paprika Chicken Schnitzel with Fried Eggs (Holstein) is a traditional German dish that features breaded and fried chicken cutlets topped with a paprika sauce and a fried egg. The chicken is pounded thin, then coated in flour, beaten egg, and breadcrumbs, and pan-fried until crispy and golden brown.

Ingredients (4 Servings)

4 boneless, skinless chicken breasts
Black pepper, to taste
Salt, to taste
½ cup all-purpose flour
2 large eggs, beaten
1 cup breadcrumbs
1 teaspoon sweet paprika
¼ cup vegetable oil
4 large eggs, for frying
Lemon wedges, for serving

Preparation

Season the chicken breasts with black pepper and salt. Put the flour in one shallow dish, the beaten eggs in another, and the breadcrumbs mixed with paprika in a third. Coat each chicken breast in the flour, then dip in the beaten eggs, and coat in the breadcrumb mixture. Heat the oil in a suitable skillet over medium-high heat. Place the coated chicken breasts to the skillet and cook until golden brown, about 3-4 minutes per side. Remove the chicken from the skillet and drain on paper towels. In the same skillet, fry the eggs to your desired degree of doneness. Serve the chicken schnitzel hot with the fried eggs on top and lemon wedges on the side. Enjoy!

Venison Loin on Schupf Noodles

Preparation time: 10 minutes
Cook time: 25 minutes
Nutrition facts (per serving): 455 Cal (12g fat, 28g protein, 3g fiber)

Venison Loin on Schupf Noodles is a traditional German dish that features roasted or grilled venison loin served with schupf noodles. Venison loin is a cut of meat from the back of the deer, which is prized for its tender, juicy, and flavorful meat. The venison is seasoned with salt and pepper and then roasted or grilled until it's cooked to the desired level of doneness.

Ingredients (4 Servings)

4 venison loin steaks, about 6 ounces each

Black pepper, to taste

Salt, to taste

2 tablespoons vegetable oil

2 medium onions, thinly sliced

2 cloves garlic, minced

1 cup beef broth

½ cup sour cream

2 tablespoons chopped fresh parsley

1 lb. schupfnudeln (German-style potato noodles)

Preparation

Season the venison loin steaks with black pepper and salt. Heat the oil in a suitable skillet over medium-high heat. Add the venison loin steaks to the skillet and cook until browned on both sides and cooked to your desired degree of doneness, about 4-5 minutes per side. Remove the venison from the skillet and set aside. Add the onions and garlic to the skillet and cook until soft, about 5 minutes. Pour in the beef broth to the skillet and cook to a boil. Reduce heat to low and stir in the sour cream and parsley. Cook the schupfnudeln according to the package instructions. Serve the venison loin steaks on top of the schupfnudeln, with the sauce spooned over the top.

Egg Noodles with Mushrooms

Preparation time: 10 minutes
Cook time: 12 minutes
Nutrition facts (per serving): 396 Cal (8g fat, 18g protein, 2g fiber)

Egg Noodles with Mushrooms is a simple and comforting dish that features tender egg noodles and sautéed mushrooms. The egg noodles are boiled until tender and then drained, while the mushrooms are sliced and sautéed in a mixture of butter, oil, or both until tender and juicy. The two are then combined in the pan, and the dish is seasoned with salt and pepper to taste.

Ingredients (4 Servings)

1 lb. egg noodles
2 tablespoons butter
2 cloves garlic, minced
8 oz. mushrooms, sliced
Black pepper, to taste
Salt, to taste
2 tablespoons all-purpose flour
2 cups chicken broth
1 cup heavy cream
2 tablespoons chopped fresh parsley
Grated Parmesan cheese, for serving

Preparation

Cook the egg noodles as per the package instructions. Drain and set aside. In a suitable skillet, melt the butter over medium heat. Add the garlic and mushrooms to the skillet and cook until the mushrooms are tender, about 5 minutes. Season with black pepper and salt to taste. Stir in the dry flour and cook for 1 minute. Gradually add the chicken broth and heavy cream, stirring constantly, until the prepared mixture comes to a boil. Reduce heat to low and cook on a simmer until the sauce has thickened, about 5 minutes. Stir in the parsley. Serve the egg noodles topped with the mushroom sauce and grated Parmesan cheese. Enjoy!

Sauteed Fish with Sauerkraut

Preparation time: 10 minutes
Cook time: 20 minutes
Nutrition facts (per serving): 421 Cal (7g fat, 22g protein, 6g fiber)

Sauteed Fish with Sauerkraut is a classic dish that features sautéed fish fillets combined with sauerkraut, a traditional German side dish made from fermented cabbage. The fish fillets are seasoned and then sautéed in a pan with butter, oil, or both until they are golden and crispy on the outside and flaky and tender on the inside.

Ingredients (4 Servings)
4 fish fillets (such as cod, haddock, or halibut)
Black pepper, to taste
Salt, to taste
Flour, for dusting
2 tablespoons butter
1 large onion, diced
2 cloves garlic, minced
1 cup chicken broth
2 cups sauerkraut, drained and rinsed
2 tablespoons chopped fresh parsley

Preparation
Season the fish fillets with black pepper and salt and dust with flour. In a suitable skillet, melt the butter over medium heat. Add the fish fillets to the skillet and cook until golden brown on both sides and cooked

through, about 4-5 minutes per side. Remove the fish from the skillet and set aside. Toss in the onion and garlic to the skillet and cook until soft, about 5 minutes. Stir in the chicken broth and sauerkraut. Cook to a boil, then reduce heat to low and cook on a simmer until the sauce has thickened, about 10 minutes. Stir in the parsley. Serve the sauteed fish with the sauerkraut on the side. Enjoy!

Red Duck Curry

Preparation time: 10 minutes
Cook time: 30 minutes
Nutrition facts (per serving): 417 Cal (12g fat, 31g protein, 4g fiber)

Red Duck Curry is a dish that features tender pieces of duck meat cooked in a flavorful, spicy red curry sauce. The sauce is made from a blend of aromatic spices and chilies, along with coconut milk and other ingredients such as shallots, garlic, ginger, and lemongrass.

Ingredients (4 Servings)
4 duck breasts, skin removed and diced
2 tablespoons vegetable oil
2 medium onions, chopped
4 cloves garlic, minced
2 tablespoons red curry paste
1 can (14 oz.) coconut milk
1 cup chicken broth
2 tablespoons fish sauce
2 tablespoons brown sugar
2 tablespoons lime juice
Black pepper, to taste
Salt, to taste
Fresh cilantro leaves, for serving
Rice, for serving

Preparation

Heat the oil in a suitable saucepan over medium-high heat. Add the duck to the saucepan and cook until browned on all sides, about 5 minutes. Remove the duck from the saucepan and set aside. Add the onions and garlic to the saucepan and cook until soft, about 5 minutes. Add the red curry paste and continue cooking for 1 minute. Add the coconut milk, chicken broth, fish sauce, brown sugar, and lime juice to the saucepan. Cook to a boil, then reduce heat to low and cook on a simmer for 10 minutes. Stir in the duck and continue to simmer until the duck is cooked through, about 10 minutes. Season with black pepper and salt to taste. Serve the red duck curry over rice and garnished with cilantro leaves. Enjoy!

Stuffed Green Peppers with Tomato

Preparation time: 10 minutes
Cook time: 35 minutes
Nutrition facts (per serving): 376 Cal (20g fat, 21g protein, 2g fiber)

Stuffed Green Peppers with Tomato is a classic comfort food dish that typically consists of large green bell peppers that are hollowed out, filled with a savory mixture of ground meat, rice, and spices, and then baked in a flavorful tomato sauce.

Ingredients (4 Servings)
4 large green bell peppers
1 lb. ground beef or turkey
1 large onion, chopped
2 cloves garlic, minced
1 can (14 oz.) diced tomatoes
1 cup cooked rice
1 teaspoon dried oregano
Black pepper, to taste
Salt, to taste
1 cup grated cheddar cheese
Tomato sauce, for serving

Preparation
At 375 degrees F, preheat your oven. Chop the tops off the bell peppers and remove the seeds and membranes. In a suitable skillet, cook the ground beef or turkey over medium heat until browned. Toss in the

onion and garlic to the skillet and cook until soft, about 5 minutes. Stir in the diced tomatoes, rice, oregano, salt, and pepper. Fill each bell pepper with the beef mixture. Place the stuffed bell peppers in a 9x13 inch baking dish. Pour the tomato sauce over the stuffed bell peppers. Sprinkle the grated cheddar cheese over the top of the tomato sauce. Bake in the oven for 30-35 minutes, or until the cheese is melted and the bell peppers are tender. Serve the stuffed green peppers with extra tomato sauce on the side. Enjoy!

Chicken with Tomato and Apple Balsamic Vinegar

Preparation time: 10 minutes
Cook time: 25 minutes
Nutrition facts (per serving): 418 Cal (14g fat, 41g protein, 3g fiber)

Chicken with Tomato and Apple Balsamic Vinegar is a flavorful and delicious dish that typically consists of chicken breasts that are seared in a hot pan and then simmered in a sauce made from juicy tomatoes, crisp apples, and tangy balsamic vinegar.

Ingredients (4 Servings)
4 boneless, skinless chicken breasts
Black pepper, to taste
Salt, to taste
2 tablespoons olive oil
1 large onion, chopped
4 cloves garlic, minced
2 medium tomatoes, chopped
2 medium apples, peeled and chopped
2 tablespoons balsamic vinegar
2 tablespoons chopped fresh basil

Preparation
Season the chicken breasts with black pepper and salt. In a suitable skillet, heat the olive oil over medium heat. Add the chicken breasts to the skillet and cook until browned on both sides and cooked through, about 6-7

minutes per side. Remove the cooked chicken from the skillet and set aside. Add the onion and garlic to the skillet and cook until soft, about 5 minutes. Stir in the tomatoes and apples and cook until the apples are soft, about 5 minutes. Stir in the balsamic vinegar and cook for 1 minute. Stir in the basil. Serve the chicken with the tomato and apple balsamic sauce on the side. Enjoy!

Austrian Bean Stew with Sausages

Preparation time: 10 minutes
Cook time: 35 minutes
Nutrition facts (per serving): 422 Cal (13g fat, 20g protein, 2g fiber)

Austrian Bean Stew with Sausages is a traditional dish from Austria that consists of a hearty stew made with beans and a variety of sausages. The stew is typically slow-cooked to develop deep, rich flavors and tenderize the ingredients.

Ingredients (6 Servings)
2 tablespoons vegetable oil
4 medium onions, chopped
4 cloves garlic, minced
4 medium carrots, chopped
2 lbs. sausages, sliced
4 cups chicken broth
2 cans (15 oz) white beans, drained and rinsed
2 tablespoons tomato paste
1 teaspoon dried thyme
Black pepper, to taste
Salt, to taste
Fresh parsley leaves, for serving
Rye bread, for serving

Preparation

Heat the oil in a suitable pot over medium heat. Add the onions and garlic to the pot and cook until soft, about 5 minutes. Stir in the carrots and sausages and cook until the sausages are browned, about 5 minutes. Stir in the chicken broth, white beans, tomato paste, and thyme. Bring the prepared mixture to a boil, then reduce heat to low and cook on a simmer for 20 minutes. Season with black pepper and salt to taste. Serve the bean stew with fresh parsley leaves and rye bread on the side. Enjoy!

Venison with Chanterelles in Cream Sauce and Red Cabbage

Preparation time: 10 minutes
Cook time: 1 hour 15 minutes
Nutrition facts (per serving): 441 Cal (13g fat, 21g protein, 4g fiber)

Venison with Chanterelles in Cream Sauce and Braised Red Cabbage is a classic game dish from Austria that features tender, juicy pieces of venison (deer meat) served with sautéed chanterelle mushrooms in a rich cream sauce and a side of sweet and tangy braised red cabbage.

Ingredients (4 Servings)
2 lbs. venison steak
Black pepper, to taste
Salt, to taste
2 tablespoons vegetable oil
2 large onions, chopped
2 cloves garlic, minced
2 lbs. chanterelle mushrooms, sliced
2 cups chicken broth
1 cup heavy cream
2 tablespoons chopped fresh thyme

Braised Red Cabbage
1 large head red cabbage, shredded
2 tablespoons butter
1 large onion, chopped

2 cups red wine

2 cups chicken broth

2 tablespoons brown sugar

2 tablespoons apple cider vinegar

Black pepper, to taste

Salt, to taste

Preparation

Season the venison steak with black pepper and salt. In a suitable skillet, heat the oil over medium heat. Add the venison steak to the skillet and cook until browned on both sides and cooked to your desired degree of doneness, about 6-7 minutes per side. Remove the venison from the skillet and set aside. Add the onions and garlic to the skillet and cook until soft, about 3 minutes. Stir in the chanterelle mushrooms and cook until soft, about 5 minutes. Stir in the chicken broth, heavy cream, and thyme. Bring the prepared mixture to a boil, then reduce heat to low and cook on a simmer for 10 minutes. Serve the venison with the chanterelle cream sauce and braised red cabbage on the side.

Braised Red Cabbage

In a suitable pot, heat the butter over medium heat. Add the onion to the pot and cook until soft, about 5 minutes. Stir in the shredded red cabbage, red wine, chicken broth, brown sugar, and apple cider vinegar. Bring the prepared mixture to a boil, then reduce heat to low and cook on a simmer for 30-40 minutes, or until the cabbage is tender. Season with black pepper and salt to taste. Enjoy!

Vegetable Soup with Sweet Basil

Preparation time: 10 minutes
Cook time: 30 minutes
Nutrition facts (per serving): 339 Cal (8g fat, 10g protein, 5g fiber)

Vegetable Soup with Sweet Basil is a soup made with a variety of fresh, seasonal vegetables and flavored with sweet basil. The vegetables can vary depending on personal preference, but common ingredients include carrots, tomatoes, onions, and potatoes.

Ingredients (6 Servings)

2 tablespoons olive oil
2 large onions, chopped
4 cloves garlic, minced
4 medium carrots, chopped
4 stalks celery, chopped
2 large potatoes, diced
4 cups vegetable broth
2 cans (14.5 oz) diced tomatoes
2 zucchinis, chopped
1 cup fresh or frozen green beans
2 cups fresh basil leaves, chopped
Black pepper, to taste
Salt, to taste

Preparation

In a suitable pot, heat the olive oil over medium heat. Add the onions and garlic to the pot and cook until soft, about 5 minutes. Stir in the carrots, celery, and potatoes and cook until soft, about 5 minutes. Stir in the vegetable broth, diced tomatoes, zucchinis, and green beans. Bring the prepared mixture to a boil, then reduce heat to low and cook on a simmer for 20 minutes, or until the vegetables are tender. Stir in the basil leaves and season with black pepper and salt to taste. Serve the vegetable soup hot, with a crusty bread on the side, if desired. Enjoy!

Veal Medallions with Caramelized Apples

Preparation time: 10 minutes
Cook time: 25 minutes
Nutrition facts (per serving): 443 Cal (20g fat, 9g protein, 1g fiber)

Veal medallions with caramelized apples is a dish made of thin slices of veal (usually from the loin) that are pan-fried or grilled to a tender, juicy finish. The medallions are typically seasoned with salt, pepper, and other herbs and spices before cooking.

Ingredients (4 Servings)

2 lbs. veal medallions

Black pepper, to taste

Salt, to taste

2 tablespoons olive oil

4 medium apples, peeled and sliced

2 tablespoons butter

2 tablespoons brown sugar

1 cup Beeren Auslese Riesling

2 tablespoons pine nuts

2 tablespoons chopped fresh parsley

Preparation

Season the veal medallions with black pepper and salt. In a suitable skillet, heat the olive oil over medium heat. Add the veal medallions to the skillet and cook until browned on both sides and cooked to your desired degree of doneness, about 6-7 minutes per side. Remove the seared veal from the skillet and set aside. Add the sliced apples to the skillet and cook until caramelized, about 8 minutes. Stir in the butter, brown sugar, and Beeren Auslese Riesling. Bring the prepared mixture to a boil, then reduce heat to low and cook on a simmer for 10 minutes, or until the sauce has thickened. Stir in the pine nuts and parsley. Serve the veal medallions with the caramelized apple sauce on top. Enjoy!

Austrian Christmas Gebackener Karpfen

Preparation time: 10 minutes
Cook time: 15 minutes
Nutrition facts (per serving): 413 Cal (8g fat, 6g protein, 2g fiber)

Austrian Christmas Gebackener Karpfen is a traditional dish from Austria, typically served during the Christmas holiday season. It's made with a whole carp fish that's seasoned, rolled in breadcrumbs, and then fried until crispy and golden.

Ingredients (6 Servings)
1 whole carp, scaled and gutted
Salt and black pepper to taste
4 slices of white bread, crusts removed
1 onion, finely chopped
1 egg, lightly beaten
2 tablespoons white wine
2 tablespoons all-purpose flour
4 tablespoons butter
Fresh parsley, chopped for garnish
Lemon wedges, for serving

Preparation
Rinse the carp inside and out and pat dry with paper towels. Season both the inside and outside with black pepper and salt. In a suitable bowl, soak the bread in water until soft, then squeeze out the excess moisture. Add

the onion, egg, and white wine to the bread and mix to combine. Stuff the prepared mixture inside the cavity of the carp. In a shallow dish, spread the flour and roll the stuffed carp in it to coat. Heat the butter in a suitable skillet over medium heat. Add the coated carp and cook, turning occasionally, until browned on all sides, about 10-15 minutes. Transfer the carp to a serving platter and keep warm. Garnish with fresh parsley and serve with lemon wedges on the side. Enjoy!

Desserts

Rice Pudding

Preparation time: 10 minutes
Cook time: 23 minutes
Nutrition facts (per serving): 299 Cal (5g fat, 4g protein, 3g fiber)

Rice pudding is a sweet dessert made from cooked rice, milk, sugar, and spices such as cinnamon and vanilla. It's often topped with raisins, nuts, or fruit and can be served hot or cold.

Ingredients (6 Servings)

1 cup long grain white rice
4 cups whole milk
½ cup granulated sugar
½ teaspoon vanilla extract
¼ teaspoon salt
¼ teaspoon ground cinnamon, optional
1 cup heavy cream
2 large eggs
Raisins or chopped nuts, to taste

Preparation

Rinse the rice and drain well. In a suitable saucepan, combine the rice, milk, sugar, vanilla extract, salt, and cinnamon (if using). Cook this mixture over medium heat, stirring constantly, until it comes to a boil. Reduce the heat to low, cover the saucepan with a tight-fitting lid, and cook on a simmer for 20 minutes until the rice is tender and the mixture is thick and creamy. Stir in the cream. In a small bowl, lightly beat the eggs. Gradually stir about 1 cup of the hot rice mixture into the eggs. Pour the egg mixture back into the saucepan and cook over low heat, stirring constantly, for 2 to 3 minutes, or until the mixture thickens. Remove the saucepan from the heat and let the pudding cool. Stir in the raisins or chopped nuts (if using). Serve warm or chilled. Enjoy!

Sterz

Preparation time: 10 minutes

Cook time: 20 minutes

Nutrition facts (per serving): 280 Cal (6g fat, 4g protein, 4g fiber)

Sterz is a traditional South Tyrolean dish that's made from a type of toasted or fried barley or cornmeal. It's a staple food in the region and is often served as a side dish, but it can also be a main dish when served with cheese, meat, or other toppings.

Ingredients (6 Servings)

2 cups of barley or cornmeal

4 cups of water

Salt, to taste

Cheese, meat, or other toppings, to taste

Preparation

Heat 4 cups of water and a pinch of salt to a boil in a medium-sized pot. Slowly add 2 cups of barley or cornmeal, stirring constantly to prevent lumps from forming. Reduce its heat to low and continue to stir for about 10-15 minutes or until the prepared mixture thickens. Remove this pot from the heat and let the prepared mixture cool for a few minutes. Shape the prepared mixture into small patties or balls. Heat a skillet over medium-high heat and add a small amount of oil. Fry the Sterz patties or balls in the skillet, turning occasionally, until they are golden brown and crispy on the outside. Serve the Sterz warm with a sprinkle of cheese or toppings of your choice.

Kardinalschnitter

Preparation time: 10 minutes
Cook time: 20 minutes
Nutrition facts (per serving): 304 Cal (4g fat, 10g protein, 5g fiber)

Kardinalschnitter is a traditional Austrian pastry made from a rich butter dough and filled with a sweet cherry or apricot filling. The pastry is often shaped like a bishop's hat or "mitre" and is named after the red color of a cardinal's hat.

Ingredients (6 Servings)

10 oz. flour

6 oz. butter, room temperature

3 ½ oz. sugar

1 egg

1 egg yolk

½ teaspoon of vanilla extract

Pinch of salt

Filling

10 oz. of cherries or apricot, pitted and pureed

2 tablespoons of sugar

1 tablespoon of cornstarch

1 teaspoon of lemon juice

Preparation

In a suitable-sized mixing bowl, combine the flour, butter, sugar, egg, egg yolk, vanilla extract, and salt. Knead the prepared dough until it becomes smooth and forms a ball. Wrap this prepared dough in plastic wrap and refrigerate for at least 30 minutes. At 350 degrees F, preheat your oven. In a separate bowl, mix together the cherries or apricot puree, sugar, cornstarch, and lemon juice. Roll out the chilled dough on a lightly floured surface to about ⅛ inch thickness. Cut the prepared dough into circles or rectangles, depending on the desired shape. Place a spoonful of the filling on one half of the prepared dough and fold the other half over to make a half moon shape. Pinch the edges to seal the pastry and brush the top with beaten egg yolk. Bake the Kardinalschnitter in the preheated oven for 15-20 minutes or until golden brown. Let the pastries cool before serving.

Punschkrapfen

Preparation time: 10 minutes
Cook time: 40 minutes
Nutrition facts (per serving): 320 Cal (10g fat, 8g protein, 2g fiber)

Punschkrapfen is a traditional Austrian pastry made from a yeast dough and filled with a rum-soaked raisin filling. It's served as a dessert or a sweet snack and is a popular treat during the Christmas season.

Ingredients (8 Servings)
1 lb. flour
1 package of active dry yeast
¼ cup of lukewarm milk
¼ cup of sugar
¼ cup of butter
1 egg
1 egg yolk
1 teaspoon of vanilla extract
Pinch of salt

Filling
½ cup of raisins
¼ cup of rum
¼ cup of sugar
1 tablespoon of lemon juice

Preparation

In a suitable-sized mixing bowl, combine the flour, yeast, milk, sugar, butter, egg, egg yolk, vanilla extract, and salt. Knead the prepared dough until it becomes smooth and forms a ball. Cover the prepared dough and let it rise in a warm place for about 1 hour or until it has doubled in size. In a separate bowl, soak the raisins in rum for at least 30 minutes. Drain the raisins and mix in the sugar and lemon juice. Roll out the prepared dough on a lightly floured surface to about 3mm thickness.

Cut the prepared dough into circles or rectangles, depending on the desired shape. Place a spoonful of the filling on one half of the prepared dough and fold the other half over to make a half moon shape. Pinch the edges to seal the pastry and brush the top with beaten egg yolk. Place the Punschkrapfen on a baking sheet and let them rise for another 20 minutes. At 350 degrees F, preheat your oven. Bake the Punschkrapfen in the preheated oven for 15-20 minutes or until golden brown. Let the Punschkrapfen cool before serving.

Shokolade Palatschinke

Preparation time: 10 minutes
Cook time: 6 minutes
Nutrition facts (per serving): 312 Cal (11g fat, 7g protein, 2g fiber)

Shokolade Palatschinke is a traditional Austrian dessert that consists of a thin, crepe-like pancake filled with melted chocolate. The pancake is folded over the chocolate to form a sandwich, and is then often dusted with powdered sugar and served with fresh fruit or a fruit compote.

Ingredients (8 Servings)
2 cups all-purpose flour
2 large eggs
2 tablespoons sugar
½ teaspoon salt
1 ½ cups milk
4 oz. dark chocolate, chopped
2 tablespoons unsalted butter
Powdered sugar, for dusting

Preparation
In a suitable-sized bowl, whisk together the flour, eggs, sugar, salt, and milk until smooth. In a separate bowl, melt the chocolate and butter together in the microwave or over a double boiler. Stir the melted chocolate mixture into the batter. Heat a large non-stick skillet over medium heat. Pour ¼ cup of the batter into the skillet and cook until golden brown on both sides, about 2-3 minutes per side. Repeat with the

remaining batter. Serve the palatschinke hot, dusted with powdered sugar and topped with your favorite toppings, such as fresh fruit, whipped cream, or chocolate sauce. Enjoy!

Thousand Cream Strudel (Millirahmstrudel)

Preparation time: 10 minutes
Cook time: 40 minutes
Nutrition facts (per serving): 440 Cal (12g fat, 6g protein, 1.4g fiber)

Millirahmstrudel, also known as "Thousand Cream Strudel," is a traditional Austrian pastry made with a delicate, flaky pastry dough and a creamy filling made with milk, cream, and sugar.

Ingredients (12 Servings)
Dough
3 cups of all-purpose flour
½ teaspoon of salt
½ cup of warm water
¼ cup of vegetable oil

Filling
2 cups of whole milk
1 cup of heavy cream
½ cup of sugar
3 egg yolks
2 tablespoons of cornstarch
1 teaspoon of vanilla extract

Brushing
1 egg yolk
1 tablespoon of milk

Preparation

In a suitable-sized mixing bowl, combine the flour and salt. Slowly add in the warm water and oil, kneading the prepared dough until it becomes smooth and elastic. Cover the prepared dough and let it rest for at least 30 minutes. In a separate saucepan, heat the milk, cream, and sugar over medium heat until it comes to a simmer. In another bowl, mix the egg yolks, cornstarch, and vanilla extract. Slowly pour the egg mixture into the saucepan, stirring constantly until the prepared mixture thickens. Remove from heat and let it cool.

Roll out the prepared dough on a lightly floured surface as thin as possible, until it becomes translucent. Spread the cooled filling evenly over the prepared dough, leaving a ⅔ inch border around the edges. Carefully roll up the prepared dough, starting from one of the long sides, into a tight spiral. Place the prepared strudel on a baking sheet and brush the top with the beaten egg yolk and milk. At 350 degrees F, preheat your oven. Bake your prepared strudel in the preheated oven for 30-40 minutes or until golden brown. Let the strudel cool before slicing and serving.

Strauben

Preparation time: 10 minutes
Cook time: 30 minutes
Nutrition facts (per serving): 320 Cal (8g fat, 7g protein, 1g fiber)

Strauben is a traditional Austrian dessert made from thin, fried dough and often filled with jam, fruit, or nuts. The dough is usually shaped into a round or oval shape and then fried until golden brown.

Ingredients (6 Servings)
1 cup all-purpose flour
¼ cup sugar
¼ teaspoon salt
¼ teaspoon nutmeg
¼ teaspoon cinnamon
¼ cup warm milk
1 egg
¼ cup melted butter
Oil, for frying

Preparation
In a suitable-sized mixing bowl, combine the flour, sugar, salt, nutmeg, and cinnamon. In a separate bowl, beat the egg and add it to the dry ingredients along with the warm milk and melted butter. Mix until a smooth dough forms. Let the prepared dough rest for at least 30 minutes. Heat oil in a suitable skillet or deep fryer to 350 degrees F. Roll the prepared dough out to about ¼ inch thickness and cut into desired

shapes. Carefully place the prepared dough pieces in the hot oil and fry until golden brown. Remove the Strauben from the oil and drain on paper towels. Serve warm with powdered sugar or your desired toppings.

Wachauer Marillenknödel

Preparation time: 10 minutes

Cook time: 10 minutes

Nutrition facts (per serving): 311 Cal (10g fat, 9g protein, 2g fiber)

Wachauer Marillenknödel is a traditional Austrian dish made with apricot dumplings.

Ingredients (6 Servings)

1 lb. apricots

1 cup breadcrumbs

½ cup sugar

¼ cup milk

2 eggs

2 tablespoons butter

2 tablespoons flour

1 teaspoon vanilla extract

Pinch of salt

Flour, for dusting

Powdered sugar, for dusting

Preparation

Pit and quarter the apricots. In a suitable mixing bowl, combine the breadcrumbs, sugar, milk, eggs, butter, flour, vanilla extract, and salt. Mix well. Form the prepared mixture into small dumplings, about the size of a golf ball. Place a piece of apricot in the center of each dumpling and press the prepared dough around it to enclose the apricot. Dust the dumplings with flour and gently drop them into a pot of boiling water. Cook the dumplings for about 8-10 minutes or until they float to the surface. Carefully remove the dumplings from the water and dust them with powdered sugar. Serve and enjoy.

Topfentorte

Preparation time: 10 minutes

Cook time: 40 minutes

Nutrition facts (per serving): 370 Cal (13g fat, 6g protein, 3g fiber)

Topfentorte is a traditional German dessert made with a crust of shortcrust pastry and a filling of quark cheese and fruit.

Ingredients (6 Servings)

1 lb. quark cheese

½ cup sugar

1 teaspoon vanilla extract

2 eggs

2 tablespoons cornstarch

½ cup sour cream

½ cup heavy cream

1 shortcrust pastry

1 lb. mixed berries or other fruit

Powdered sugar, for dusting

Preparation

At 350 degrees F, preheat your oven. Roll out your shortcrust pastry and line a 9-inch (23cm) pie dish with it. In a suitable mixing bowl, combine the quark cheese, sugar, vanilla extract, eggs, cornstarch, sour cream, and heavy cream. Mix well. Spread the quark mixture over the shortcrust pastry in the pie dish. Arrange the mixed berries or other fruit on top of the quark mixture. Bake the torte for 35-40 minutes or until the crust is golden brown and the filling is set. Remove the baked torte from the oven and let it cool completely. Dust the torte with powdered sugar before serving.

Reindling

Preparation time: 10 minutes
Cook time: 35 minutes
Nutrition facts (per serving): 361 Cal (9g fat, 2g protein, 2g fiber)

Reindling is a traditional German dessert made with a yeast dough and a filling of raisins and cinnamon.

Ingredients (6 Servings)

½ cup warm milk
2 ¼ teaspoon active dry yeast
¼ cup sugar
¼ cup butter
2 eggs
1 teaspoon salt
3 cups all-purpose flour
½ cup raisins
2 teaspoon cinnamon
Powdered sugar, for dusting

Preparation

In a suitable-sized bowl, combine the warm milk and yeast. Let it sit for about 5 minutes until the yeast is activated and the prepared mixture becomes frothy. In a suitable-sized mixing bowl, combine the sugar, butter, eggs, salt, and activated yeast mixture. Mix well. Gradually add in the flour, one cup at a time, until the prepared dough comes together. Turn the prepared dough out onto a lightly floured surface and knead it for about 8-10 minutes until it becomes smooth and elastic. Place the prepared dough in a greased bowl, cover it with a towel, and let it rise in a warm place for about 1 hour.

At 350 degrees F, preheat your oven. In a suitable-sized bowl, combine the raisins and cinnamon. Roll out the prepared dough on a lightly floured surface into a rectangle about ¼ inch thick. Sprinkle the raisin mixture over the prepared dough, leaving a 1-inch border around the edges. Roll up the prepared dough tightly, starting from the long end. Place the roll in a greased loaf pan and let it rise for another 30 minutes. Bake the reindling for about 30-35 minutes or until it's golden brown. Remove the reindling from the oven and let it cool completely. Dust the reindling with powdered sugar before serving.

Topfenstrudel

Preparation time: 10 minutes
Cook time: 40 minutes
Nutrition facts (per serving): 360 Cal (14g fat, 4g protein, 1g fiber)

Topfenstrudel, also known as Quark Strudel, is a traditional Austrian dessert made with a phyllo dough and a filling of quark cheese, sugar and raisins.

Ingredients (6 Servings)

2 cups quark cheese
½ cup sugar
¼ cup raisins
1 teaspoon vanilla extract
2 egg yolks
¼ cup heavy cream
¼ cup flour
Pinch of salt
1 package of phyllo dough (about 16 sheets)
¼ cup melted butter
Powdered sugar, for dusting

Preparation

At 375 degrees F, preheat your oven. In a suitable mixing bowl, combine the quark cheese, sugar, raisins, vanilla extract, egg yolks, heavy cream, flour, and salt. Mix well. Spread out one sheet of phyllo dough on a clean surface and brush it with melted butter. Repeat with 5 more sheets of phyllo dough, brushing each sheet with butter. Spread the quark mixture over the phyllo dough, leaving a 1-inch border around the edges. Roll up the phyllo dough tightly, starting from the long end. Place the prepared strudel on a baking sheet lined with parchment paper. Brush the top of the strudel with the remaining melted butter. Bake the strudel for about 30-40 minutes or until it's golden brown. Remove the baked strudel from the oven and let it cool for a few minutes. Dust the strudel with powdered sugar before serving.

Salzburger Nockerl

Preparation time: 10 minutes
Cook time: 25 minutes
Nutrition facts (per serving): 296 Cal (14g fat, 4g protein, 2g fiber)

Salzburger Nockerl is a traditional Austrian dessert made from a light and fluffy souffle-like mixture.

Ingredients (6 Servings)

6 egg whites
6 egg yolks
½ cup sugar
¼ cup flour
¼ teaspoon salt
Powdered sugar, for dusting

Preparation

At 350 degrees F, preheat your oven. In a suitable-sized mixing bowl, beat the egg whites with an electric mixer until stiff peaks form. In a separate mixing bowl, beat the egg yolks with an electric mixer until they become pale yellow. Gradually add in the sugar, flour, and salt to the egg yolks while continuing to beat. Gently fold the egg yolk mixture into the egg whites. Grease a baking dish with butter or oil. Pour the prepared mixture into the baking dish, and create three peaks on the surface. Bake the nockerl for about 20-25 minutes or until it's golden brown on top. Remove the nockerl from the oven and let it cool for a few minutes. Dust the nockerl with powdered sugar before serving.

Germknödel

Preparation time: 10 minutes
Cook time: 20 minutes
Nutrition facts (per serving): 300 Cal (16g fat, 7g protein, 1g fiber)

Germknödel is a traditional Austrian dessert consisting of a large, fluffy dumpling filled with plum jam, topped with melted butter and poppy seeds.

Ingredients (6 Servings)
Dough
1 ½ cups flour
¼ cup sugar
¼ teaspoon salt
½ cup warm milk
1 egg
2 tablespoons melted butter
1 package of active dry yeast

Filling
1 cup of plum jam

Topping
¼ cup melted butter
2 tablespoons poppy seeds

Preparation

In a suitable mixing bowl, combine the flour, sugar, and salt. In a separate mixing bowl, combine the warm milk, egg, melted butter, and yeast. Mix the wet mixture into the dry flour mixture and mix until a dough forms. Knead the prepared dough for about 8-10 minutes, until it becomes smooth and elastic. Place the prepared dough in a greased bowl, cover it with a towel and let it rise for about 1 hour. Roll out the prepared dough into a large rectangle, about ¼ inch thick. Spread the plum jam over the prepared dough, leaving a 1-inch border around the edges. Roll up the prepared dough tightly, starting from the long end. Cut the roll into slices, about 2 inches thick. Place the Germknödel slices in a pot of boiling water and let them cook for about 15-20 minutes or until they float to the surface. Remove the Germknödel from the water and let them cool for a few minutes. Brush the Germknödel with melted butter and sprinkle with poppy seeds. Serve and enjoy!

Kaisersemmel

Preparation time: 10 minutes
Cook time: 25 minutes
Nutrition facts (per serving): 288 Cal (12g fat, 9g protein, 2g fiber)

Kaisersemmel is a type of bread roll that is popular in German-speaking countries such as Germany, Austria, and Switzerland. It's named after the Austro-Hungarian emperor Franz Joseph I and is characterized by its round shape with a crispy crust and soft interior.

Ingredients (8 Servings)

1 lb. all-purpose flour
⅓ teaspoon active dry yeast
¼ teaspoon salt
¼ teaspoon sugar
1 ½ cups warm water
2 tablespoons oil
1 egg yolk
1 cup milk
Poppy seeds, to taste

Preparation

In a suitable-sized mixing bowl, combine flour, yeast, salt and sugar. Gradually add warm water and oil to the prepared mixture while stirring. Knead the prepared dough on a floured surface for 10 minutes or until smooth. Place the prepared dough in a greased bowl, cover, and let it rise for 1 hour. At 450 degrees F, preheat your oven. Divide the prepared dough into 8-12 equal parts, roll into buns, and place on a baking sheet. Brush buns with egg yolk and milk mixture, sprinkle with poppy seeds. Bake for 20-25 minutes or until golden brown. Serve hot. Enjoy!

Drinks

Viennese Hot Christmas Punch

Preparation time: 10 minutes
Nutrition facts (per serving): 108 Cal (0g fat, 0g protein, 1g fiber)

Viennese Hot Christmas Punch is a traditional warm alcoholic beverage that is popular in Austria during the Christmas season. It's made from a mixture of red wine, mulling spices (such as cinnamon, cloves, and nutmeg), sugar, lemon, and sometimes brandy or rum.

Ingredients (12 Servings)

2 liters of red wine

4 cups of cranberry juice

2 cups orange juice

10 oz. sugar

4 cinnamon sticks

8 cloves

2 sliced oranges

2 sliced lemons

2 sliced limes

Preparation

In a suitable pot, combine wine, cranberry juice, orange juice, sugar, cinnamon sticks, and cloves. Add sliced oranges, lemons, and limes. Heat over low heat, stirring occasionally until sugar has dissolved. Serve hot in mugs or heatproof glasses. Optional: garnish with a slice of orange or lemon.

Jagertee

Preparation time: 10 minutes
Cook time: 10 minutes
Nutrition facts (per serving): 112 Cal (0g fat, 1g protein, 3g fiber)

Jägertee is a popular German alcoholic beverage made from black tea, rum, and spices. It's traditionally consumed during the colder months and is often served at Christmas time.

Ingredients (12 Servings)

4 cups of black tea
2 cups of dark rum
2 cups of red wine
8 oz. of sugar
2 cinnamon sticks
4 cloves
4 allspice berries
2 star anise
1 sliced orange
1 sliced lemon

Preparation

In a suitable pot, brew black tea and let it cool. Add rum, red wine, sugar, cinnamon sticks, cloves, allspice berries, and star anise. Add sliced orange and lemon. Heat the prepared mixture over low heat, stirring occasionally until the sugar has dissolved. Serve hot in mugs or heatproof glasses. Optional: garnish with a slice of orange or lemon. Enjoy!

Austrian Hussar

Preparation time: 10 minutes
Nutrition facts (per serving): 118 Cal (1g fat, 1g protein, 2g fiber)

Austrian Hussar is also the name of a cocktail, typically made with equal parts of brandy and cherry brandy, mixed with a small amount of lemon juice. It is typically served in a cocktail glass and garnished with a cherry.

Ingredients (2 Servings)
2 oz apricot brandy
1 oz gin
1 oz orange juice
1 oz lemon juice
1 oz grenadine
Dash of egg white
Orange twist, for garnish

Preparation
Fill a shaker with ice. Add apricot brandy, gin, orange juice, lemon juice, grenadine, and egg white. Shake well until fully combined and frothy. Strain into a chilled cocktail glass. Garnish with an orange twist. Enjoy!

Gluehwein

Preparation time: 10 minutes
Cook time: 10 minutes
Nutrition facts (per serving): 117 Cal (0g fat, 4g protein, 2g fiber)

Glühwein is a traditional German warm, spiced wine drink. It is made from red wine, cinnamon, cloves, nutmeg, star anise, and sugar, which are heated and served in a mug.

Ingredients (8 Servings)
1 bottle of red wine
1 cup of sugar
2 cinnamon sticks
4 cloves
4 allspice berries
2 star anise
1 sliced orange
1 sliced lemon

Preparation
In a suitable pot, combine wine, sugar, cinnamon sticks, cloves, allspice berries, and star anise. Add sliced orange and lemon. Heat the prepared mixture over low heat, stirring occasionally until the sugar has dissolved. Serve hot in mugs or heatproof glasses. Optional: garnish with a slice of orange or lemon. Enjoy!

Einspänner

Preparation time: 10 minutes
Nutrition facts (per serving): 119 Cal (0g fat, 2g protein, 2g fiber)

Einspänner is a traditional Viennese coffee drink that consists of a single shot of espresso served in a glass with whipped cream. The whipped cream is usually flavored with a small amount of liqueur, such as Grand Marnier or Kirschwasser, and is topped with a dusting of cocoa powder.

Ingredients (2 Servings)
¼ cup heavy whipping cream
2 teaspoon granulated sugar
⅛ teaspoon kosher salt
2 cups ice cubes
1 cup cold-brewed coffee
Cocoa powder, for garnish

Preparation
In a suitable bowl, beat the cream, sugar and salt until thickened and airy but far before peaks form. It should be decidedly thinner than whipped cream and have the consistency of melted ice cream: silky, light and pourable. Divide the ice and coffee between two (12-ounce) tumbler glasses. Pour the cream into each glass and, through a fine-mesh sieve or with your fingertips, lightly dust with cocoa powder.

If you liked Austrian recipes, discover to how cook DELICIOUS recipes from **Balkan** countries!

Within these pages, you'll learn 35 authentic recipes from a Balkan cook. These aren't ordinary recipes you'd find on the Internet, but recipes that were closely guarded by our Balkan mothers and passed down from generation to generation.

Main Dishes, Appetizers, and Desserts included!

If you want to learn how to make Croatian green peas stew, and 32 other authentic Balkan recipes, then start with our book!

Order at www.balkanfood.org/cook-books/ for only $2,99!

Maybe Hungarian cuisine?

If you're a **Mediterranean** dieter who wants to know the secrets of the Mediterranean diet, dieting, and cooking, then you're about to discover how to master cooking meals on a Mediterranean diet right now!

In fact, if you want to know how to make Mediterranean food, then this new e-book - "The 30-minute Mediterranean diet" - gives you the answers to many important questions and challenges every Mediterranean dieter faces, including:

- How can I succeed with a Mediterranean diet?
- What kind of recipes can I make?
- What are the key principles to this type of diet?
- What are the suggested weekly menus for this diet?
- Are there any cheat items I can make?

... and more!

If you're serious about cooking meals on a Mediterranean diet and you really want to know how to make Mediterranean food, then you need to grab a copy of "The 30-minute Mediterranean diet" right now.

Prepare **111 recipes with several ingredients in less than 30 minutes**!

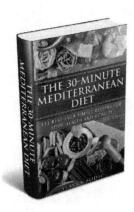

Order at www.balkanfood.org/cook-books/ for only $2,99!

What could be better than a home-cooked meal? Maybe only a **Greek** homemade meal.

Do not get discouraged if you have no Greek roots or friends. Now you can make a Greek food feast in your kitchen.

This ultimate Greek cookbook offers you 111 best dishes of this cuisine! From more famous gyros to more exotic *Kota Kapama* this cookbook keeps it easy and affordable.

All the ingredients necessary are wholesome and widely accessible. The author's picks are as flavorful as they are healthy. The dishes described in this cookbook are "what Greek mothers have made for decades."

Full of well-balanced and nutritious meals, this handy cookbook includes many vegan options. Discover a plethora of benefits of Mediterranean cuisine, and you may fall in love with cooking at home.

Inspired by a real food lover, this collection of delicious recipes will taste buds utterly satisfied.

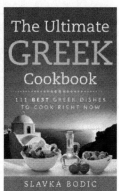

Order at www.balkanfood.org/cook-books/ for only $2,99!

Maybe some Swedish meatballs ?

Maybe to try exotic **Syrian** cuisine?

From succulent *sarma*, soups, warm and cold salads to delectable desserts, the plethora of flavors will satisfy the most jaded foodie. Have a taste of a new culture with this **traditional Syrian cookbook**.

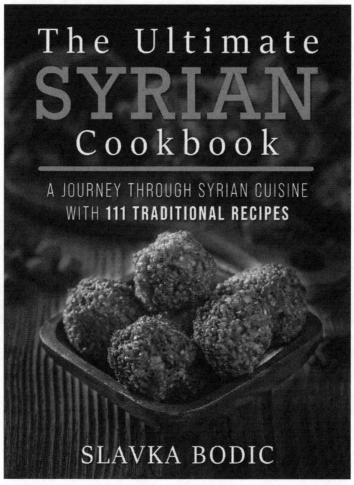

Maybe **Polish** cuisine?

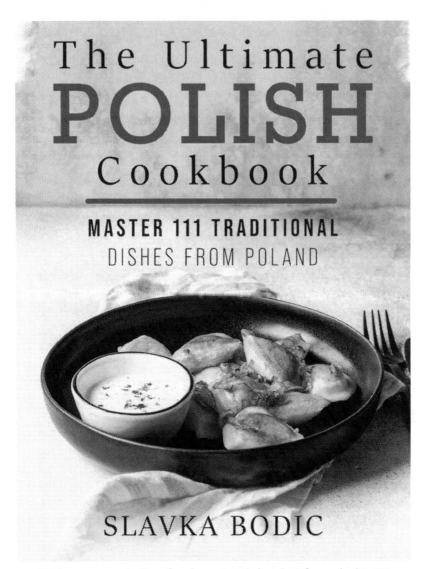

Order at www.balkanfood.org/cook-books/ for only $2,99!

Or **Peruvian**?

ONE LAST THING

If you enjoyed this book or found it useful, I'd be very grateful if you could find the time to post a short review on Amazon. Your support really does make a difference and I read all the reviews personally, so I can get your feedback and make this book even better.

Thanks again for your support!

Please send me your feedback at

www.balkanfood.org

Made in the USA
Columbia, SC
03 May 2024

5f5ac61f-9e5b-4c53-ab16-d2276049bb1dR01